GENESIS

PETER GABRIEL, PHIL COLLINS AND BEYOND

GENESIS

PETER GABRIEL, PHIL COLLINS AND BEYOND

PHILIP KAMIN · PETER GODDARD

INTRODUCTION BY PHIL COLLINS

Beaufort Books

New York/Toronto

Published in the United States by Beaufort Books
9 East 40th Street, New York, New York 10016

Library of Congress Cataloguing in Publication Data

Kamin, Philip.
   Genesis : Peter Gabriel, Phil Collins & beyond.

   1. Genesis (Musical group) 2. Rock groups — England.
I. Gabriel, Peter. II. Collins, Phil. III. Goddard,
Peter. IV. Title.
ML421.G46K3 1984   784.5'4'00922 [B]   84-9308
ISBN 0-8253-0243-9

Design by David Wyman

Printed and bound in Canada

INTRODUCTION

There are always three or four very familiar
faces one sees when one looks out into an
audience. These familiar faces are usually in
the section known as the "photo pit." One of
these faces belongs to Phil Kamin. He takes
photographs. In fact, he takes great photographs. Inside this book is a collection of pic-
tures taken at various concerts with various
personnel in various disguises. From Milton
Keynes to Milwaukee, he always seems to
appear and has become a close friend over the
years. With Peter Goddard as a partner, they
have captured a few of the many reasons why
Genesis was formed and exists today. Enjoy it.

Phil Collins
Guilford, Surrey
May 6, 1984

PART ONE

REUNION CONCERT 1982

"For all that, we will try to give them what they want — a bit of nostalgia."

*— Peter Gabriel
at the Genesis Reunion Concert*

It was in England and it was raining — a vintage Genesis day. There was something of the quality of a medieval fair to it as people slogged into Milton Keynes Concert Bowl — earth, rain and rainbows of colors. Peter Gabriel pulled up backstage with his family in the car. The old costumes were in the trunk and back seat.

And standing together in a tight circle were Phil Collins, Mike Rutherford, Tony Banks and...there was Steve Hackett. Well now, to anyone who might be observing the goings-on, it was the reunion Genesis fans had been waiting for.

There were T-shirts, programs, buttons and sweat-shirts: "Six Of The Best" they read. "Milton Keynes Concert Bowl, Saturday 2 October, 1982."

It was like an extended family getting back together again. Around noon, still under that grey English sky, it began. John Martyn, Blues Band and Talk Talk were the opening acts. The rain kept coming. Then, at the edge between evening and night, Jonathon King made his way to the stage to talk about this young band that had shown up one day. It was still dreary when Peter Gabriel was carried onstage in a white coffin, and a huge cheer went up.

The reunion concert began with *Back in N.Y.C.*

Old friends kept bumping into old friends. A woman met a former lover. They'd been Genesis fans right from the start but their spouses weren't, so they'd each come alone. They began to talk about their marriages and their kids and where you could find the softest nappies. And they ended up holding hands.

People had come from Italy and France, Southern California and Aukland, New Zealand, Canada and Sweden. Armando Gallo, one of the band's longest lasting fans and its chronicler, was shooting photos up onstage. Another long-time Genesis observer, Philip Kamin — the one who indeed, takes these photos — was in the pit in front of the stage.

And it was from that vantage point he noticed something odd. The only time the rain stopped was during the performance of *Supper's Ready*. Was this some sort of sign?

Probably not.

No, no, maybe years ago it might have been like that; you know, with signs and magic and stuff like that. But this was *now*. This was business in its way. This was a benefit. It was a gift from Genesis to Peter Gabriel to help him cover the debts incurred by his WOMAD festival earlier that year.

"It was a festival designed to integrate Third World music with rock," Gabriel had told me only a few weeks before the benefit. "We had 600 amateur musi-

cians from twenty-one countries — from China, Egypt and Tunisia — and it had a fantastic educational side to it with 7000 school kids coming in to experiment with all these new instruments and to play along with drummers from different countries."

We were in his hotel room. It was half a year since I'd last seen him perform, and I suppose my memory of the performance had heightened its eerie aspect. I was expecting — despite, I should note, all I knew to the contrary — the character, not its creator.

Peter Gabriel seems to inhabit a no-man's land on stage — a strange place that's sometimes ghastly, sometimes childish or brutal or shocking. In this room, with all its beiges and muted personality, he might have been the young university professor explaining a research project he'd come up with for one of his brighter classes. There was, after all, that certain donnish tone in his voice: slightly ironic, gently fun, deliberate:

"It was a fantastic three days," he went on about WOMAD, "but it lost a pile of money. Genesis very kindly offered to do the gig with me to help pay the costs the festival ran up. We're making no bones about what the concert's all about. It's our means of getting our fingers on the cash we need — about 200,000 pounds."

It had been seven years since they had all worked together though, he knew. "I've got new cassettes and lyric sheets to try and teach myself all the stuff that I've forgotten," he reflected. "For all that, we will try to give them what they want — a bit of nostalgia."

What they were going to give was what Genesis had been.

Philadelphia, 1981: It was dark and chilling, a typical night-on-the-road, and a typical night for the new Genesis.

As the limo eases down into the back entrance to the Spectrum, it passes a clump of fans who peer through its dark windows looking for rock stars. Except there's a problem: The kids know who they're looking for, all right, but they don't exactly know what they look like.

This band, I find myself thinking, is rock's secret success story. It's survived a decade and a half of rock's stormiest years as well as the loss of two key members, no small accomplishment in itself; and each year its popularity, as registered by record sales, has increased. Each new album tends to sell more copies than the last.

Still, its three key members have remained somewhat anonymous. Front man Phil Collins, keyboard player Tony Banks and guitarist-bassist Mike Rutherford aren't names widely known to the *People* magazine reading public at large. It's not "Mick! Bette! and heeeere's... Tony!" No, not yet.

There are no Genesis scandals, no punch-ups in hotel bars, no television sets flying through fourteenth-storey windows. "News of the World" hasn't dwelled on their sex lives. At least in print.

Even the emergence of Phil Collins as a solo act — an enormously successful and highly public solo act at that — has done little to change this. Perhaps this rankles the three men from Genesis, I don't know. It doesn't seem to. Quite the opposite, it seems to suit them well.

They talk a lot about emotion and gut reaction — about laying their feelings on the line when they write and record songs. There's even some anger which flares up now and then when critics label them an "intellectual" band.

"All they are saying is that we're not like a straight rock'n'roll band, really," Mike had told a *Dallas Morning News* reporter.

"We're not the cerebral band people think we are. We work from the gut. Always have."

– Mike Rutherford

But the outsider sees them differently than they see themselves. He hears the feeling in the music, certainly. But that's not what he finds in first meeting them. Then, it seems to him, it's their easy intelligence that gets them through. Their manners. Their civility.

Most others in rock'n'roll who have gone as far as Genesis has, have something of the survivor about them: it was the risks, bloody enormous risks in some cases, which in some weird way paid off but left visible scars behind.

Not so with Genesis. The risks for them were just as bloody enormous — the pressure on marriages, careers, hopes and health, the kids not seen as they grew up. But they've somehow been taken in stride — the feelings those risks generated have been absorbed within the band itself. They've hidden the scars.

Besides, the outsider has the sense that it's not over yet; that they've not felt they've arrived yet; that they're still working it out.

There is, of course, the positive side to all this anonymity. Genesis is one of the few long-lived bands known by what it actually *sounds* like.

"Hold it, stop here," Collins tells the limo driver. It's the second of Genesis' three sold-out filled-to-capacity concerts — and all you hear on local rock radio is the band's pointed and punchy new music.

Several of us get out and walk back to the people waiting around, but it's not until Collins is up close that they sort him out from the rest of the crowd. Quickly, it's darting hands and fast smiles. It's "sign this" and "do you remember playing that?" But they're not awed by him, not really. It's as if, well — as if they feel comfortable with him. What they're in awe of is what he's done.

A little later.

Tony Smith, the band's manager, is being filmed. The camera and sound crew sneak into every conversation we have.

Genesis is "thinking about" a concert movie, Smith says, and these scenes "might and might not" be part of it. After debating for years whether or not to film itself — and having suffered through seeing an early Genesis-in-concert movie they hated — they've decided to take a stab at it. Their main worry is not image but quality of images.

"What the younger bands are after," Smith goes on, "is a street image. All that '50s and early '60s look. They wanted to be really 'street,' whatever that is."

An ambling, bearded man constantly in search of a cigarette, he remains remarkably unpressured in a position which automatically brings on high blood pressure. He doesn't shield Genesis from the outside world, he explains, and that's why the band's been able to remain relatively untouched by the money and/or fame that has come its way.

"We're not street," he adds, staring down a camera lens. "We're more...avenue.

"That's it. We're really avenue, man."

A quick history shows that they're also decidedly well adjusted, well educated middle-class. Genesis' genesis came at Charterhouse, a public school near Godalming, Surrey. Two school bands, The Anon and the Garden Wall, were blended to form the first Genesis early in 1967. Various personnel changes later yielded the lineup that first became known in North America: Banks, Rutherford and lead singer Peter Gabriel, the three original schoolmates, plus Collins, then the band's drummer, and guitarist Steve Hackett.

To many, Genesis was Gabriel. His wildly extravagant costumes, with bats' wings and flower-petal hats, represented the fullest flowering of late-'60s rock's penchant for lushness and fantasy. Yes, King Crimson, Gentle Giant and Rush, among many other bands, were all fed on this imagination, much the way David Bowie, Alice Cooper and others were nourished by its darker side. Genesis was the gentlest of them all. Gabriel's grotesques never frightened. They were friendly goblins.

He decided to quit for a solo career during the band's North American tour for *The Lamb Lies Down on Broadway* album and it was assumed the band's loss was irreparable. But it wasn't, nor was it much affected when Hackett decided to leave shortly after. The remaining members simply called their next album *Then There Were Three*, which was released in March 1978, and when the band went out on tour again it had two full-time sidemen: guitarist Daryl Stuermer who replaced Hackett, and drummer Chester Thompson arrived to allow Collins to sing.

Even the individual solo records which have since followed — Collins' *Face Value* album perhaps being the most commercially successful — have done little to stop the band's relentless schedule and, it appears, inevitably growing success.

Still later.

Crates holding their two travelling pingpong tables have yet to be unpacked. Genesis plays a lot of pingpong on the road — a throwback to all the squash played at Charterhouse?

"There's nothing terribly complex about us," says Tony during a break before they go up onstage at one end of what is in appearance a huge woofer designed to accommodate a hockey rink.

"We play contemporary music. The point of the music we write is that it is to be enjoyed at the particular time and it's irrelevant what people will think of it in five years' time."

We're sitting in a circle in a cramped little dressing room and I have the strange feeling we're having something like a Boy Scout meeting.

I'm struck by their patience. "People do have this misconception of us," says Mike Rutherford. "We're

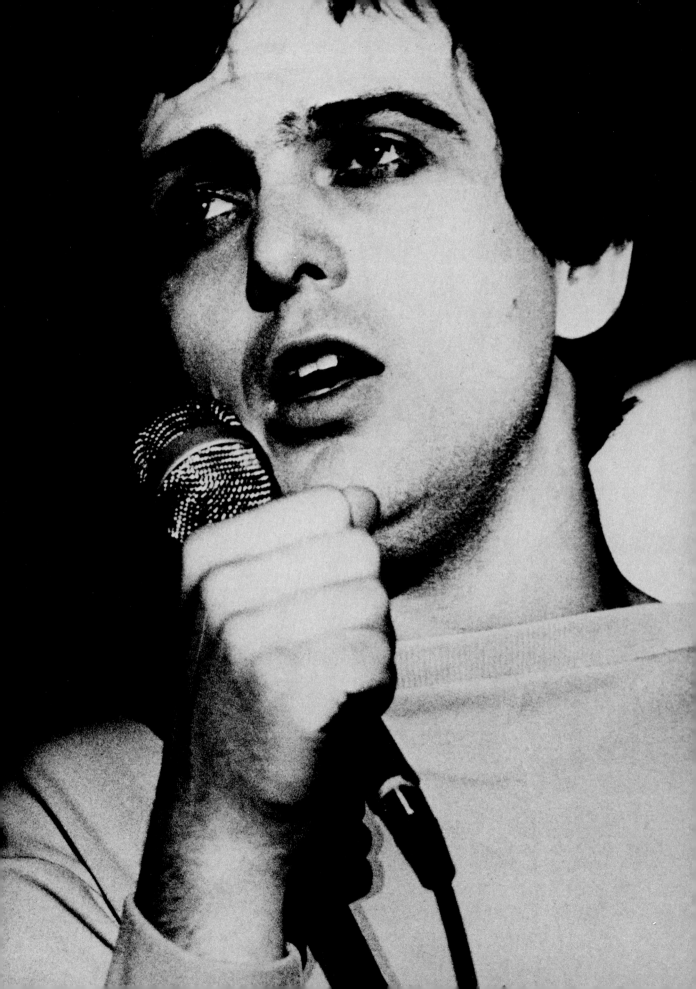

not the cerebral band people think we are. We work from the gut. Always have.''

Banks stiffens. He has something to say.

Intense and self-critical, the words dash out as if he fears he'll never have enough time to say all he has to say. Rutherford, tall and easygoing, seems to be the middle-man in their group dynamic. Collins, one senses, is more instinctive than the others.

''What has always kept it interesting for me are these contrasts within the group,'' Banks says. ''I would hate just to be called a 'heavy metal' band and only do that. I like some of it, but just to do that would be very boring.''

''There's something interesting about our audience,'' Rutherford says. ''Some will like one side of what we do and nothing else. And there are others who'll like the opposite. They'll both be there, though.''

Abacab, the album just out then, came about from what Collins calls ''a bit of a rebellion in the band.'' They were tired of having others produce them and now had a chance to do it themselves. Then again, as Tony Smith explains, they've always needed something to struggle with; that, in fact, Genesis originally became a band only because the individual song writers couldn't find anyone else to play their material.

Rutherford notes: ''I seriously think that if we hadn't worked on our own, outside the group, we wouldn't be together today. Some musicians do it because they're not happy with what they're doing inside the band. With us, we all write quite a lot. One Genesis album a year is not enough of an outlet, so we go elsewhere.''

PART TWO
MIKE RUTHERFORD AND TONY BANKS

"Perhaps the only group which did appeal to us and which was current at that time would have been King Crimson."

– Tony Banks

We've gone down the road a bit. Tony Banks and Mike Rutherford sit on the couch talking about their lives together. They're so different in so many ways — Tony's dark, quick, direct, intense, not about to be hemmed in; Mike's bright, easier going, gentle. It's these very contrasts which most likely have allowed them to work together for so long.

But there are ties here that bind. There are the ties to the whole idea of what Genesis is. They'll tell you about the group songs, the ones everyone brings something to like *Supper's Ready* and *Abacab*, which are among the most successful things they've done.

Talk to Phil Collins and you'll hear about these ties. He's particularly conscious of the entire group idea, maybe because his own solo success has made him think about and reconsider his links with the band.

But there's something deeper that runs between Tony Banks and Mike Rutherford than the idea of Genesis. It has something to do with their background — both born in 1950 and growing up in comfortable families; both going to prep and public schools yet being part of that generation of young British men who had come to realize that tradition alone would not be to their advantage; both loving music and having parents who encouraged their love; both coming to rock'n'roll from well outside its own traditions, yet coming for all the right reasons because they *had* to play it.

For Genesis to have lasted from the 1960s through to the 1980s has been the result of much happy circumstance and some good fortune. Phil Collins, soon after joining the band, became frustrated by all the attention being paid to Peter Gabriel's costumes. Collins was with another band, Brand X, and possibly would have left Genesis completely had not Gabriel told everyone that he'd be the one who was going to leave. (Gabriel's own press release from mid-1975 named among the other *non*-reasons for leaving: "to do a 'Bowie'...to do a 'Ferry'...to do a 'Furry Boa' and hang myself with it.")

But here too the band may have ground to a finish if everyone had immediately fretted about replacing Gabriel. Instead, they did what they'd done before in that winter of 1969 when they'd decided once and for all they were going to be a band — they started to write songs.

Back then they'd settled into an isolated cottage an hour's drive north of London that had been loaned to them by a friend, Richard MacPhail. After Gabriel's departure they weren't nearly so isolated — the press, after all, wanted to know what was going on — but the writing seemed to come easier. The new material turned out to be *A Trick of the Tail*.

Perhaps the transition from the Genesis with Gabriel to the one without him might not have gone as smoothly or successfully as it did had it not been for the odd coincidence that Phil Collins' voice just happened to sound so much like that of the former singer's.

There are other "ifs" and "perhapses" on all of this, but what kept everything on line was Rutherford and Banks. They are the cogs and gears and wheels of the band.

And they had to rely on each other because they were outsiders. "I think in the very early days we were outside the way things were normally done," says Mike. "I think one thing that helped us is that when we decided to go do it professionally we spent this long period of time on our own.

"We did an awful lot of writing then. We were learning how to write together and play as a band. We were very new to the music business. And I think because we were so insular we developed our own ideas. And even during that first year of touring we remained outside the way things were normally done. I think it sort of set us off on that road a bit. It had nothing to do with fashions or trends."

Tony sits back a bit and adds: "I think also that at that particular time, when we were starting off, we didn't like most of the music of that particular era. There were a few people that we liked. But we'd been influenced much more by some earlier groups — the Beatles and the Kinks and the Animals — and there some people who influenced us. But we didn't really like the kind of things that were around at the time.

"Bubblegum music and blues music were the two main things then, and neither particularly appealed to us. Perhaps the only group which did appeal to us and which was current at that time would have been King Crimson.

"In a sense we were just trying to find different things to do by ourselves because we didn't find what other people were doing that interesting. And we found we could get away onstage with doing a kind of complicated music. We found we were slowly building up an audience."

"Something tells me you'll always be outsiders, to one degree or another," I say. "Even now, with all the commercial success."

It's a pale mid-winter afternoon and the sun is white and without much heat.

"Definitely the band has a different approach to its music," says Tony. "In one way, we have always gone after the same thing — which is to make music that is first pleasurable to ourselves. And we hope that other people are going to like it. That's always been the way we worked and there's no real difference now. That's the way we do it and the way we always did it. The way of going about it may be slightly different now I suppose, but the motives are the same."

"But the sound is much sparer now compared to the way it was," I tell him. "Leaner. Tougher. Is it because you know more about recording techniques or have you changed your attitudes toward what you're playing?"

"Well," says Tony, "there was a reasonably conscious attempt at the time of *Abacab* to try to avoid what we

felt were becoming Genesis cliches; the sort of big keyboard sounds, the standard solos, the tambourine on the chords — that kind of thing. That was the kind of thing we'd done for ten years. We thought, 'Let's just try doing it a different way.'

"But we've developed some more since then. I think on our newer albums, the ones after *Abacab*, we've gone back to some of the earlier textures. So again we have yet another slightly different approach to the music.

"I think there's now a nice combination of some of the old and the new, of some of the older feel with some of the new harder edge. We get this combination from the way we work. We also get it with the engineer we now use who gets a harder sound."

"I agree," says Mike. "I don't feel there's been a change of approach. But right now we're in the position, musically I mean, that we could go anywhere. The next album could take us anywhere."

This is the way it was at the start, I find myself thinking.

"We were always playing in places which didn't know us. But then it became a great buzz because you'd go and play a town, sometimes for the first time…and suddenly you'd click with the audience."
— Mike Rutherford

They were schoolboy song writers wanting to make the best impression they could when Jonathan King, a Charterhouse old boy himself, booked them into the Regent A studio in London late in 1967. Their first release, arriving in February 1968, was the single *Silent Sun*. Its flip side was *That's Me*. The release of their first album, *From Genesis To Revelation*, occurred in March, 1969. Soon after that they made the crucial decision: they were going to become musicians.

Until then, the lineup had included, besides Gabriel, Banks and Rutherford (who switched to bass after playing guitar in the Anon), singer-guitarist Anthony Phillips and drummer John Silver who replaced Chris Stewart. By the end of the following year yet another drummer would join — John Mayhew. It wasn't until 1970, after Tony Stratton-Smith signed the band to his new label, Charisma, would the lineup be settled for a while. Ant Phillips left the band in July 1970 after they'd finished recording *Trespass*. It now counted Phil Collins and guitarist Steve Hackett as members.

I wondered out loud, "Maybe two distinct Genesis audiences have developed. There's one which exists only for the earlier records because of the lushness of the lyrical imagery, and there's one that's brand new. I mean, in North America I'm sure, two-thirds of the people really don't know your earlier work."

Tony replies: "That depends upon what you mean by early work. You know, in a sense we've publicized those earlier albums and we've sold a lot of them since the group's gotten more popular. And this is great as far as we're concerned because we're proud of those early albums.

"But, you know, for most of the North American audience — it's probably more true in the States than it is in Canada in a way, though — the band kind of began in the late '70s. That was when the change came."

"I've been amazed, though," says Mike. "I mean, I've been noticing over the last few nights how the younger kids too who were cheering the old stuff. And they can't have been around then."

Tony: "There's something else we've found on the latest tours. I think a lot of the audience found itself hearing music it had not been aware of at all in any form or another. Yet this music went down very well. I think it went down well because of the strength of the songs themselves and the way they sounded onstage. I mean, the songs that we do — the old songs we do onstage, things like *The Carpet Crawlers* — well, there's no particular reason why they go down so well other than the basic reason that people just like them. Some people are aware of some of the old songs I think because they were publicized on *Three Sides Live*. That album helped a lot, but old songs mean different things to different people."

He's being very deliberate here. At school he was good at maths and sciences and you can sense he's one of those rare musicians who doesn't mind analysing what he does.

"We always say 'old songs' and 'new songs,'" he goes on. "But for some people, younger fans, what I mean by 'old songs' includes everything — *Abacab* and anything else before that. For some people it even includes our newer albums, I think. When you're saying that this is a new song, a lot of people think you mean it's something they've never heard before. It's always true to say that the most recent album goes down the least well. It's always been that way. But even here I noticed a change: the newer albums are better and better received."

Mike: "*Abacab* went down very well right from the first time around."

"It was probably as close as you've gotten to something very…well, current in a hit parade sense," I suggest. "I mean, Genesis was always somewhere outside the hit parade mentality."

Tony: "We still *are* outside. Take *Abacab*. It's not as simple as it might seem to be. It's a deceptively straightforward song, I think. But I think it still is unusual in its way. It still doesn't sound like anyone else. It's a Genesis song. There's no one else you could say that sounds like."

PG: "I suppose it was what Peter was doing way back that has made everyone always expect something completely different from you. I mean, Peter was beyond belief. Bizarre…"

Tony: "It was not really that bizarre. It had its own

logic. You're looking at it the wrong way. What happened was that we got onstage with a total PA system. We were singing lyrics which were fairly complicated because we found it easier to write complicated lyrics than simple lyrics. And we found that when you're singing songs that have a rather complex flavor you need to illustrate them in some way. So Peter started to tell stories, stories which originally had something to do with particular songs. After a bit, though, he got into his own thing.

"It developed from there. During the song we'd try to illustrate little points which we felt were strong moments in the song. We'd try to get across something in particular and there'd be something, well, like the flower mask — that was just to show that there was some sort of bizarre kind of thing going on.

"It was meant to be humorous and a bit weird. It was easy enough to do. I mean, there's nothing very clever about putting on a flower mask but it became a kind of trademark with people. It sort of evolved and over the years it got stranger and stranger things happening in that way. But it was quite logical for us really. We were just illustrating our songs."

Mike: "The only thing I didn't feel comfortable with — and I think everybody felt the same — was when he wore the red dress and the fox's head that came off."

Tony: "Then he wore his — what was it he wore? — a music box or something when it should have been the old man's mask which was obviously appropriate because that's what the song was about."

PG: "But this was the period of classic Genesis, of *Nursery Cryme* coming out in November 1971 with *The Musical Box* on it, and *Foxtrot* being released the following year with *Watcher of the Skies* and *Supper's Ready*. In December of 1972 you made your U.S. debut at New York's Philharmonic Hall as the top-billed act on WNEW-FM's annual Christmas benefit."

"It was slow for us in England at the start," Mike is remembering. "We were always playing in places which didn't know us. But then it became a great buzz because you'd go and play a town, sometimes for the first time or nearly the first time, and suddenly you'd click with the audience. And that would be the beginning of a kind of hardcore following in that town.

"And as we spent all our time in England in the early days, we just went round and round and built up on that. But still, the first time we played the place and felt the click, that was it. That was a really nice feeling. You'd never have it quite the same again."

Tony: "You must understand that those first four albums, starting with *From Genesis to Revelation* and the next three after that [*Trespass, Nursery Cryme* and *Foxtrot*] really didn't sell anything. The *Cryme* perhaps sold a little bit more than its two predecessors but it didn't do very much in England and it did nothing in North America. So for the first few years you're talking about a very few people who actually got into our music enough to go out and buy an album.

"But there were a few people who saw us and perhaps thought there was something special happening and really liked what we did. But in the main a lot of people didn't like it, to be honest."

Mike: "And can you imagine how odd we must have appeared? At the time I didn't realize it, but I saw a bit of what we were like back then and I can imagine now looking back how odd we must have appeared. We must have appeared miles and miles away from the mainstream — the mainstream of *any*thing."

"It has to be remembered," I say, "that Bowie wasn't a big name in North America at least until he decided to stop using costumes."

Tony: "Well, I think his music has gotten more straightforward over the years, you know."

"Nevertheless, I think there was some reluctance to accepting your music, as you say."

Tony: "I also think that as much as anything else, the reason we appeared to be bizarre, both visually and musically, was because we were making mistakes: it was because we were trying to get a certain kind of sound on record which we never managed to get.

"We were terribly keen — we used to overlay millions of guitars and things. And then we'd use all the tracks. So there was some stagnation in the early days. You'd have ten guitars going at the same time and you couldn't hear any of them. And the band was so low in the mix. It was all so bizarre. It was attractive in a way because it was slightly...you know, it was a very unprofessional approach. It was quite untutored if you like.

"It was the same with the entire show because we were untutored here too. Peter was anything but an actor. All the rest of us were very self-conscious onstage.

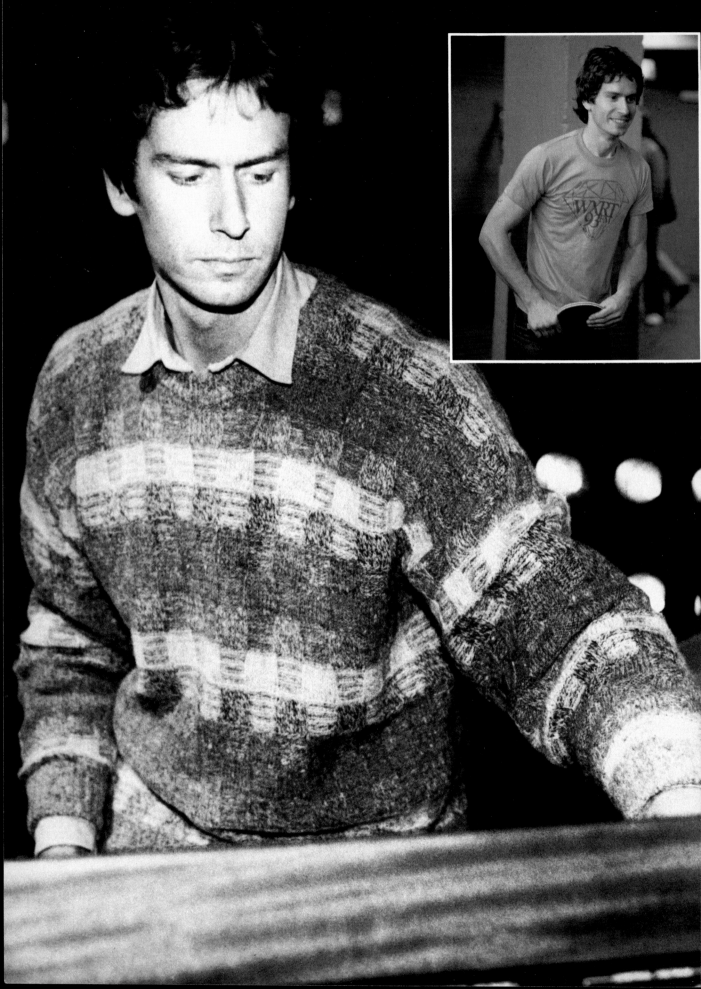

We just sort of were there. We didn't stand up there and start something, because we didn't feel that kind of confidence. We thought we were a bit weird. We were these introverted people standing there onstage, just playing music.

"Besides, when we first started out we were really anti-image of any kind. We used to go out onstage in exactly what we came to the gig in. We'd just walk out and play. There was no question of changing clothes or anything like that.

"And so it was a slow learning process for us. Not having been in the business for any length of time we had to find our own way. Now we get it right because we know how to do it now. In those days we didn't."

PG: "Was it difficult then to do the reunion concert, with the costumes and everything, because it took you back to those old, untutored days?"

Mike: "No. Not at all. It was all done for the right reasons. It was done as a charity thing to raise money. It was a 'one of' occasion and it wasn't being filmed and it wasn't being recorded. This, I think, is very important because if we were going to watch a film of it today I don't think it would live up to what we'd done before. It was very emotional. It was something that happened in the heat of the moment. We were moved by it. But I wouldn't want to watch it on TV now."

Tony: "But I think that was always true with the band in those days. We always were a far better live band than we ever were if you were to see us on television. I think it's true even now. And I think the reason we're a far better live band is because we've never looked quite right on TV.

"The TV people, whoever was doing the show, always wanted to go in for a close-up of one guy or another. Then there was the fact that Peter's makeup would look terrible when you'd get too close to it. It was convincing from a distance — that's what it was designed to do. It was very over-exaggerated. But if you saw it in a close-up it just looked terrible.

"It has to do with image. In a concert you can control the whole atmosphere you're in in terms of lighting and music and the whole thing. You're in total control of the situation, much more so than you are when there's someone with a TV camera."

Mike: "I remember seeing a close-up of Pete, once. That disturbed me, seeing that close-up on the TV screen. It was so close that Pete's face looked like some cracked moon crater. It was on there for about three minutes. He was just singing. That was so embarrassing. I think it was our live shows that really got us our following."

But it was their records that maintained their reputation. *Selling England by the Pound*, released late in 1973 to coincide with the band's second and by far biggest North American tour, and *The Lamb Lies Down on Broadway*, released in November 1974, were not merely listened to. They were analysed. There were mysteries supposedly hidden in the music and lyrics.

Three pieces was inevitable, I think. There is no band I can think of that has five people who write and have strong ideas... and which has survived as long as we have.''

— *Mike Rutherford*

The Lamb was a complex work, a musical as much as a concert concept, and Genesis performed it 107 times over a period of six months. It was a watershed work. Gabriel had hoped it would show a tougher side of the band's work. And maybe to some fans it did. To others, though, the tougher Genesis, the band with a harder sound and the more direct lyrical imagery began with *A Trick of the Tail*, which was released in February 1976.

Along the way they were beginning to reconsider the very process of composition. They wanted to make it more direct and spontaneous. And they began thinking about composing in the studio, directly onto tape.

''In the early days when we were writing albums like *Selling England by the Pound*, we used to do it with a cassette player which we kept running most of the time,'' Tony explains. ''We used to get some amazing moments on that cassette player — moments that sounded so good. Later, we'd try to recreate them in the studio and we just couldn't get them right.

''We wanted for a long time to try and do the actual writing with a twenty-four-track machine in the room with us. But *Genesis* [1984] is the first album for which we were able to do that. So we were able to capture things we had done in jam sessions — something like *Mama* for example — and get them down on tape.

''Otherwise those pieces would have vanished. They would have become overcomplicated for one thing. We'd have probably rehearsed them too many times and then we'd have lost the essence of what was good about them in the first place. And that would have been sad.

''There are many things which can be found if you listen to some of these old cassettes. They're just little ideas, the kind you think that it would have been so nice to have been able to do something with. We did try very hard on *The Lamb Lies Down on Broadway* to kind of keep all the little moods that were created at the start. But we lost the atmosphere of most of them.''

''What was the reasoning for the parting with Peter?'' I ask directly.

''I think several reasons really,'' says Mike.

''In terms of friendship, maybe there hasn't been a separation?'' I wonder.

''No, no,'' says Tony, ''we are very friendly.''

Mike: ''It was personal, though.''

Tony: ''The personal problems were, I think, actually the key thing. Being in a band does put a strain on

family life and he was the first to have children. The rest of us, Mike and I included, we were very unsympathetic to these kind of problems because we weren't in that situation. And to be honest, the band couldn't afford to take the time necessary to give someone a reasonable family life while at the same time keep the group going. We can do that now, though. We've learned how to manage. That perhaps was the fundamental reason.

"Also, I think Peter had the most obvious alternative career to go to. That meant that he could actually make that decision. Whereas if any of us did it we knew it would have been suicide. Hindsight has shown us, though, that the band had to get smaller. Hindsight has shown us that we had to get down to this."

Mike: "Three pieces was inevitable, I think. There is no band I can think of that has five people who write and who have strong ideas...and which has survived as long as we have. Right after Pete left we found that we suddenly had a lot more space to work in. That was good for a couple of years. And then Steve didn't feel he could handle the solo stuff and the group stuff as well and left. I think he was always more interested in solo stuff."

Tony: "Well, I think that he found that his writing got squeezed out a bit because of what the other four of us were doing. We seemed to prefer the stuff that Mike and I were writing to the stuff that Steve was writing. And so therefore we tended to use a bit more of our stuff than his.

"At that point Phil wasn't writing yet so that wasn't a factor. But I think there is room for the three. Musically it works. Obviously we can, between the three of us, accommodate all the instruments we need to produce our albums. So it's turned out to quite a neat unit, really."

"Your solo records always surprise me," I say. "I hear things in them I never hear in the band. And that's true even when you're playing on each other's records; it's strange."

"Which is good, I think," says Mike.

I add: "Yeah, Phil may be the only exception to it. I can see some transference to Genesis albums of what he does as a solo act on his albums."

Mike: "I think each solo record you make tends to make you go a bit further in your own direction."

Tony: "I think that when we did our different personal solo albums there was a feeling that the band then was probably more closely following my own personal tastes than it was reflecting the taste of any one of the other members. And so it wasn't surprising that the first solo album I did was fairly close to the Genesis kind of feel."

"Only it was so much darker," I suggest.

Tony: "Yeah, I definitely went down one particular road. That was the idea of the album. I wanted to concentrate in one area, rather than to try to do a couple of different things that I'd noticed the band doing. I just wanted to take one idea and take it to a

conclusion. But obviously, most of the feeling on the album was compatible with a lot of the stuff that was done with Genesis.

"I think the same is probably true with Mike's. Mike's first album certainly bore a resemblance to Genesis. But I think there's been a change in this process. There's a longer time between Genesis albums now, so individual taste has a longer time to change. I think that's one reason why the newer solo albums sound more and more different from one another than they did perhaps in the old days.

"Back then, the albums were done one after the other. The songs were being written one after the other, too, throughout the entire year. For instance, when we had a day off and we weren't doing a gig it would be a song writing day for us. We might have started the first bars of say, *Watcher of the Skies*, the day after we finished *Nursery Cryme*. That's how it was. It was a continuous operation. Some songs in those days dated back to the early cottage days. Some of these songs would appear five years after they were written."

"Is there any temptation to spread things out more, to take more time to do things?" I ask.

Mike: "When you say spreading things out, I think that's what we were already doing. We'd do a Genesis block — that would mean we'd make an album, finish it off, do all the video stuff to go with it — then we'll go away and do stuff on our own for the rest of year. I suppose Phil's got so much happening for him at the moment that I think it's difficult to spread it out too much. Besides, I feel the gaps between each new Genesis album are quite good. I like the fact that there are gaps in between.

"Still, we're fairly busy. Some of these bands just go away and for six months do nothing. That's not the way we work. There won't be many gaps with us. It won't be the case that we'll go out on tour every two or three years. Our next tour will be when the next album comes out."

Tony: "I think you'll find that the time lapse between the main albums — that's forgetting about a live album — has been about the same; the same as it was between *Abacab* and *Genesis*. There's a logic to the time frame and what it comes down to is that we're basically woring all the time — which is how we like to do it."

Mike: "Things are definitely a lot easier, though."

Tony: "You can choose what you want to do a little bit more now. In the old days we had a very regulated existence with the touring and then when you weren't actually doing a gig, you were rehearsing. I think it was far harder in those days in a way. The main difference now is that every gig, when you're on the road, every gig is very important. These days, when you're playing to ten thousand to twenty thousand people every night, it's important that you get it across the best you can. So you have to concentrate very much harder. There's definitely more of a strain to playing live now."

"As well, the playing's become a lot more emotional," I say.

Mike: "It's not a conscious thing, really. You're not looking at each other. Apart from the technical aspect and the sound, the playing now is much more emo-

tional. It's the emotion which keeps you going. It's what's noticed."

Tony: "As soon as you think about things too much, as soon as you concentrate on what you're doing too hard, it gets very difficult. The best things come when you find they just happen naturally. It's like when you're driving. Sometimes you find you've driven twenty miles without being even slightly aware of what's gone on the past twenty miles. You haven't had a crash so you assume you're all right. The best thing is to let your mind go completely blank, you know. And just…"

Mike: "The worst thing is when you have a bad moment onstage, and you can have a totally blind moment every so often. Very often during the rest of the evening or for the next half hour or hour you're thinking, 'Christ, what's going on?' And suddenly your confidence goes. You can only rely on just doing it naturally."

Tony: "That's true of everything. That's true in sports — everything. When you play games — say ping-pong — you obviously will analyse what the other guy's doing. If the other guy's put a sort of topspin on the shot you know you have to counteract that spin. So you're watching all the time what the other guy's doing.

"But the less you concentrate on it the better you seem to play. You have to let your subconscious sort of absorb what the other guy's doing and then it seems to work the best."

"But things must change ever so slightly from show to show — a little more of this one night, a little less the next night," I say.

Mike: "We don't change the set that much. It's not like some bands who improvise an awful lot. But still, one night feels different from another."

"If you're no longer rehearsing what you've put on cassette before you record, does that put more emphasis on rehearsal before a tour?"

Tony: "In rehearsing for a tour you just learn how to play the songs. There's a purely technical side to it. We'll bring Chester and Daryl back in to learn how to make the thing sound like a group."

"Were they at all intrigued by computer programming? They do have their own studio, after all."

Mike: "We're a bit the other way actually. The possibilities of the things you can do are so incredible these days, at least what you can do technically in terms of the studio. But we're going much more for a feeling. Everybody's fighting against becoming too technical. I mean, in our studio the mixing console is definitely not the top of the line of the mixing consoles but is a modest little fellow. But it does a great job. The studio's very lively. Nothing really matters as long as you can just get something down on tape then you've got it."

Tony: "Well, look at some of the Beatles' stuff, which was some of the greatest music ever recorded — it was done with a four-track machine. I think the technical stuff can help you. It can't improve on things. It just provides tools."

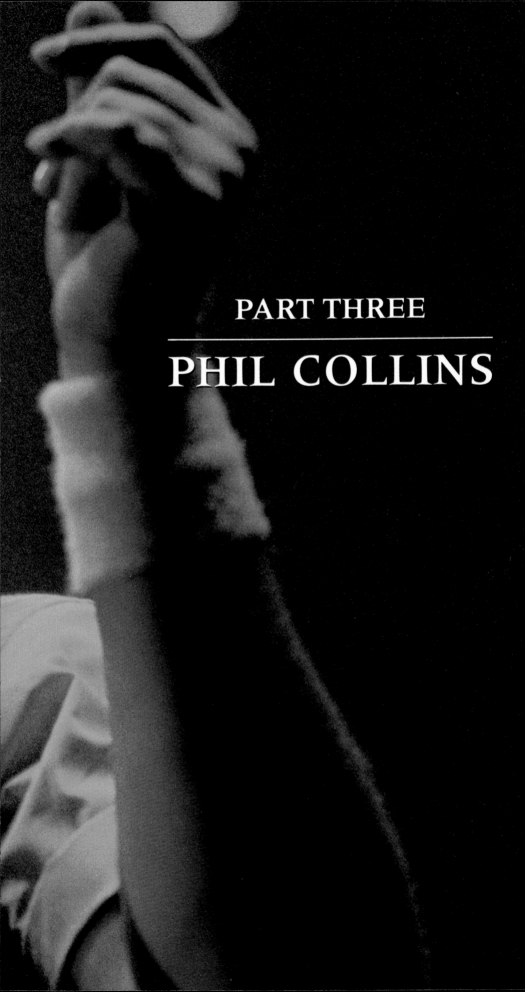

PART THREE
PHIL COLLINS

"There was no real preconception when we did *Abacab* that it was going to be a major change."

– *Phil Collins*

I am riding in a limo with Phil Collins, enjoying the cushy, smooth ride until the moment he tells me, from his corner of the dark rear seat, that he didn't like what I'd written about his first album, *Face Value*.

Suddenly the ride is a lot less smooth.

"Uh well," I begin to mumble, "well, actually, I didn't like the way the record company had tried to hype it and I hadn't..."

His expression doesn't change, but he settles back.

He didn't want to bottle his feelings up, he says. "That's why I told you."

I'm a critic, and critics have reacted variously to Genesis. But generally through the years two schools of thought have emerged — one which so admires the band's intelligence that reviews become analyses; and the other which thinks this intelligence gets in the way of show business.

I've tended toward the latter — until the more recent albums that is. I'm a Genesis revisionist, if it matters at all where I stand. I like the punch and fun of *Illegal Alien* with those overlapping chords that shift and float under Collins' voice during the song's intro — a wonderfully unsettling bit of rock'n'roll to hear these days on your car radio — but the music is not particularly profound.

I *do* think the intro to *Illegal Alien* grabs you as firmly as does the "wellllll" that kicks off Gene Vincent's *Be-Bop-A-Lula* — that the music and vocal work nicely and neatly as rock'n'roll, in other words. *This* part of Genesis I understand. In truth I never fully understood *The Lamb Lies Down on Broadway* and even developed a bit of a distrust of those fans who believed they did.

Actually, I always thought this was a much more playful band — brighter, happier even — than was ever understood. I remember being knocked back by Gabriel's costumes during one of their early North American tours, and thinking, "What a wonderfully bizarre bit of weirdness."

Here, I reflected, was the makings of the greatest stand-up costume act since Milton Berle.

I think it was the combination of Gabriel's verbal and visual extravagances and the rest of the band's reticence that came to determine the way the band came to be seen — that something impenetrably mysterious was going on. And maybe it was. But perhaps the band's real sophistication lay elsewhere, in its ability to *evolve*.

This evolution has frustrated some of its older fans, and for their sakes it's tempting to point out that the kind of short, punchy rock song Genesis is recording in the 1980s is much the kind of thing they were trying to write when they were a schoolboy band trying to impress Jonathan King.

This, remember, was a band which had learned some of its song writing from the Beatles and won its first contract by writing a Bee Gees-like song.

But that's not really what's involved here. What is involved is Phil Collins and his growing influence on the material — and the others' influence on him. He hadn't written much for the band, he explains, up until the point of a change in his personal life.

There was *Misunderstanding* and *Please Don't Ask* which appeared on *Duke*. But then his marriage broke up and he suddenly found himself with lots of extra time on his hands — song writing time. *Face Value* came from this burst of energy as did his contribution to *Abacab*.

Then, too, he was being discovered by new Genesis' audiences — not as another Peter Gabriel but as very much another kind of figure onstage. There was something fleeting about Gabriel, something shadowy and magical and mysterious surrounding what he did. In contrast, there's something definite and compact and power-packed about Collins.

If Gabriel's characters were evocative of Genesis' literary side — part comic-strip-horror cartoon, part Peter Pan, part faerie at the bottom of the old English garden — Collins underlines the British music hall, show business and rock'n'roll traditions. He's slightly younger than the others — he was born in 1951 — but he has always been very much the old pro, having drummed since he or anyone else can remember.

"A while ago," he tells me sometime after that ride, "I'd gotten hold of a tape of a film we had made with Peter. It was something I'd never seen before; it was to be released in 1973. We were doing stuff on it that went right back to *The Musical Box* and *Watcher of the Skies*. It just shows how much we've changed since.

"Mike put his finger on it. He said it's no surprise that we weren't very popular in America at that time because Peter was so far out and the rest of us were so non-visual. It's no surprise in retrospect that things took a long time.

"But do you want to know something? When we finally did the kind of music we started playing with *Abacab*, it didn't seem to us to be a risk or a departure. At least, that's not the way we looked at it. That's not the way we work. We just tried to do something different. In retrospect it's easy to say that it was a risk.

"I mean, at the time it was...well, you just follow your nose and try to do whatever you can that excites you.

"There was no real preconception when we did *Abacab* that it was going to be a major change. There was no internal thinking like, 'Right, now we're going to change things and we're gonna try to do things 'cause we're sort of fed up with the way we've become.'

"There was none of that. There was no sitting around trying to work it out to be that way."

But there was one new factor involved — the influence of Hugh Padgham. It was Padgham who strengthened the rhythm track.

"Hugh and I had worked together on Gabriel's albums [they met when Phil recorded Peter's third solo album] and we'd worked together on my things," Collins went

on. "Because of him we ended up with a monster drum sound. It took up so much space that there was less room for other musical material. This is one of the reasons why musically and texturally our music became a little sparser. With that big drum sound there was a little less room for everything else on the record. And there was less of a need for everything.

"I mean, in the old days we'd go to the other end of the scale. With *Nursery Cryme*, for instance, we rehearsed for eight weeks in a room. Everybody was playing these really thick chords and Tony had three hands on his keyboards. It was all very complex. But when we tried to reproduce that sound in the studio, when we tried to get it on record, it sounded a bit messy.

"You know, playing live you need a bit more energy than you do when you're playing under the kind of close scrutiny which goes into making a record. So we used to rehearse and rehearse *Nursery Cryme* and *Trespass* and everything we did up until *The Lamb*. We even did a lot for *The Lamb*. But *The Lamb* was probably the first decent recording we made, in terms of getting a bit of excitement on record.

"So, that was the one side of how we recorded. Now it's a very big, live sound. My drum sound alone occupies quite a lot of room."

Like Buddy Rich before him, Phil Collins came to drumming professionally after doing a bit of everything else, from dancing to acting. Rich was the kid vaudeville

"But when the situation came around where I could actually write — you know, a quiet situation where I could write and let my feelings flow through — then it all came out."

— Phil Collins

star in the 1920s who went on to be perhaps the hardest hitting drummer of the big band era — and beyond.

Collins, similarly, was the kid star who went on to be a hard-hitting no-nonsense kind of drummer. There are not many rockers who could have survived before rock came along, but he's certainly one of them.

So, to find him fronting Genesis is much less of a surprise than it appeared to be to Genesis-watchers at first. If there is any surprise, to him as well as to others, it perhaps comes with his emergence as a song writer.

"I'd done *Face Value* by the time we did *Abacab*," he goes on. "The reason why there's a bit more of me on *Abacab* is because I had a little bit more to give. I'd not really written that much. But it gets difficult here. I can see it all very clearly, the change that went on with us. But I can't describe it properly.

"Up until *And Then There Were Three* I was married with two kids and I had a lot of other responsibilities. I had to divide my time between what I had to do with my family and what I wanted to do with my musical career. The music tended to occupy a lot of space in my life but I wasn't giving everything I had to it. So when my divorce happened I then ended up with all this extra time which I was able to use. It wasn't that I wanted it to turn out this way, but suddenly I had all the time and inclination to channel my energy into something — writing songs.

"So, therefore, when it came down to the next band album after *Face Value*, which really was *Duke*, I found I could contribute more in the way of song writing. *Duke* was sort of a strange interim period for me because I had at that point decided that I was going to release my songs as an album. And so I kept most of them for my next album, apart from *Misunderstanding* and *Please Don't Ask* which ended up on *Duke*. *Duke* was probably the first album which I felt I'd given one hundred percent of myself on.

"It was great to think I actually had the time to follow things through. I had already found out with *Face Value* that I actually had more to offer than I had been offering. And it wasn't that I was being suppressed or repressed at home by family or whatever. It was just that there wasn't the time to do it. I'd been doing Brand X and various other recording sessions and at that time all these things were more important to me than writing my own music.

"But when the situation came around where I could actually write — you know, a quiet situation where I could write and let my feelings flow through — then it all came out. I actually found I enjoyed the idea of writing a lot more, too. And with *Abacab*, which was the first real major group project since my confidence-building with *Face Value*, I put a lot more of me into it. I think it was the first album that had probably thirty-three-and-a-third percent from everybody.

"This may sound strange but I thought that *Abacab* was as equal as it was going to get between us. But now, the way we work is even more equal. You know what I mean? We're closer. With Genesis we actually went into the studio to work on it. When we did *Abacab* we didn't use the studio for the writing but used the living room, and we moved into the studio for the recording.

"This is the band's studio I'm talking about. I'd used it for various products and Tony and Mike had used it for their albums, so the studio was well oiled before we started the Genesis album.

"We moved into it with no music written at all. We just had the idea that we would start mucking about — jamming or whatever you want to call it — and record at the same time. We thought we'd hone the music while we were playing it back.

"We did something like this with *The Lamb* because we recorded that album almost live in a bar in Wales. So a lot of the things on that album — songs like *The Waiting Room* and *Silent Sorrow* came out of jams. There's quite a few on that album, quite a few things were recorded because the tape was running and we just kept playing.

"Usually, the way we used to work, whatever we were working on would end up on cassette. And there we'd be, going into the studio two months later and trying to recreate what was on those cassettes.

"So with Genesis, we actually started with nothing at all written down. We just put some drum machine patterns on...I started singing, Mike started playing and Tony started playing...and things like *Mama* came out.

"This would never have happened, I think, if we had been in the other situation. Knowing the ways that we used to work — and sometimes do work — we'd end up overarranging everything or overcomplicating it. We'd often end up so that we didn't know the wood from the trees.

"This time I dragged Tony and Mike in and said, 'Listen, this is great, let's keep it a little like this.' When we first started recording this way, Tony was a little skeptical about whether the music we'd come up with would be developed enough merely by recording it as we wrote it. But what in fact happened — and I know he's happy about it now — is that all the real fears were dispelled in a couple of days.

"We didn't actually just settle for the first thing we recorded. We recorded something and then listened to it. If something was wrong, we'd say, 'Let's go back and do it again.' It was almost a better way of keeping track of all the music because you could come and listen to exactly how something was sounding. And I also think we found a way that the three of us really want to work.

"In retrospect, *Abacab* was a transition period. At the time it was the best thing we were doing. As all these new albums are, though. In each new album we are going to try to do different things — whether these are different things musically or a different way we think about what we're doing. And sometimes the music might end up sounding to somebody who has been listening to us for years the way they think Genesis should sound.

"*Dodo* is to a lot of people a very typical Genesis song. But to me and Tony and Mike, the way it was written and performed wasn't quite the same as the way we used to do things. We came up with a slightly better way of doing it.

"We don't think too much about this kind of thing. It's only when we talk about it that we start to think about it. Basically, we found a way of working on that album that for Genesis meant the group can continue to exist.

"We found a way to do something together we can't do individually."

There's an idea behind most bands or soloists in rock, I start to say, and there was a very definite idea about Genesis right at its very beginning. Whether it was ever defined or written out or talked about, there was, nevertheless, this idea. Everybody involved in the band seemed to agree with it.

But now there is another idea for the band. "The fantasy, the fairy tale, the lushness, the very Englishness of

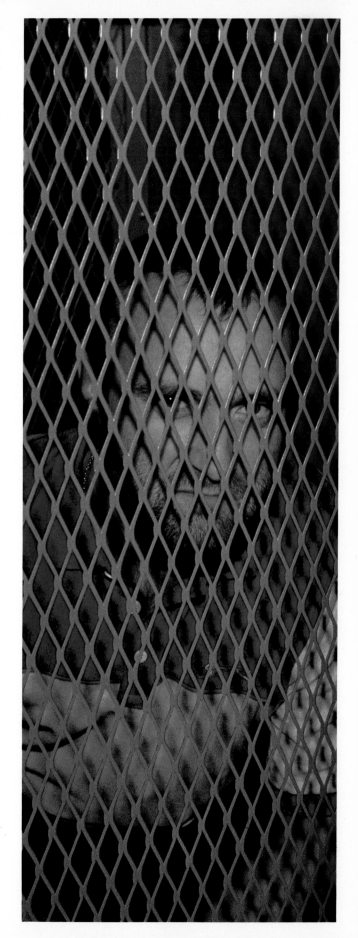

it," I say, "that was part of the original idea. Now there's a different premise behind everything."

"I think that what it is now is a totally different thing to what it was even two or three years ago," Collins says. "I don't know what it was like at the beginning, but twelve years ago there was a little less material and we were a little less together.

"The emphasis of the group used to be much more biased toward Tony and Pete and Mike, that is to say not so much toward Steve and me. Pete always wanted us to be a bit more butch, a bit tougher. But we really didn't know how to do it. I viewed our old video recently. He's really trying to be butch but he really doesn't know how to do it.

"I thought one of the last times I saw him that he was much, much better than he was when I'd seen him earlier on — better in terms of the way he performed. He was much more convincing.

"Before, it was much more of a passive thing. The lyrics were much more poetic. The lyrics probably read better than they were sung. Musically too it was much more passive. But with *The Lamb*, where Pete played a New Jersey thug, it became a bit more butch.

"Musically, we're now tougher than we were before. I mean I think we could still go onstage if we wanted to, in flowered gear or whatever, and tap dance. But the actual music would still be tougher than it was. I'm not saying that being tougher is necessarily better or whatever. To me, I prefer the music we're doing now to the music we used to do. But then we wouldn't be here now unless we had what we used to have.

"But it seems I have never really gotten out of wanting to do other things — things like touring with Robert Plant. That was a great experience. It's great fun to play another kind of music, to be honest. You know, it brings out a side of me that might not come out. It's a side of me that I haven't really been able to get out — apart from the opportunity inside the band.

"To me it was an opportunity to play a different kind of music. It was also the chance to actually play the drums again. There I was out on tour, with no other responsibilities for two months, and all I had to do is just play the drums.

"I feel better now because I've just done Robert's tour. I feel a little less pressure because I like to be thought of as a drummer. Until Robert's tour I think a lot of people had forgotten that I was a drummer.

"I listened to a lot of drummers, you know. There was the big band Buddy Rich, the swinging big band, and well, Keith Moon...and Ringo. Ringo Starr. He's a great drummer. I put on some of the old Ed Sullivan shows I managed to get hold of and I watched the Beatles early on. He's a great drummer. His stuff on *Revolver*, *Sgt. Pepper* and *Strawberry Fields Forever* was great. He's a classic rock drummer I think.

"Charlie Watts, with the Stones, is a class R & B sort of basic drummer. Ringo's far subtler in some ways than Charlie is. Charlie is great. I like his work very much. But he's even more brutal than people think Ringo is. *Strawberry Fields Forever* has got some of the best rock drumming that you'll hear. *Revolver* too.

"And the sound. Ah! That drum sound."

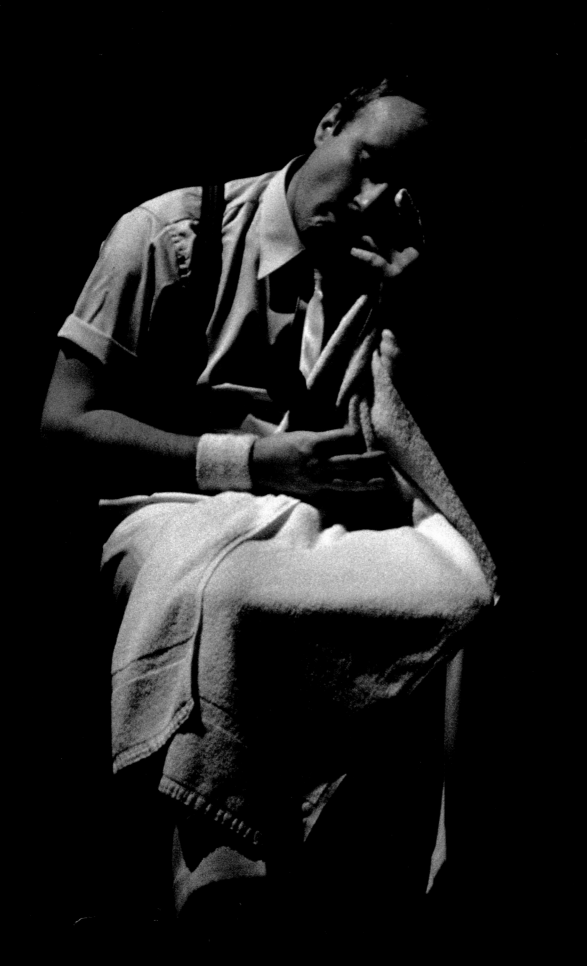

PART FOUR

PETER GABRIEL

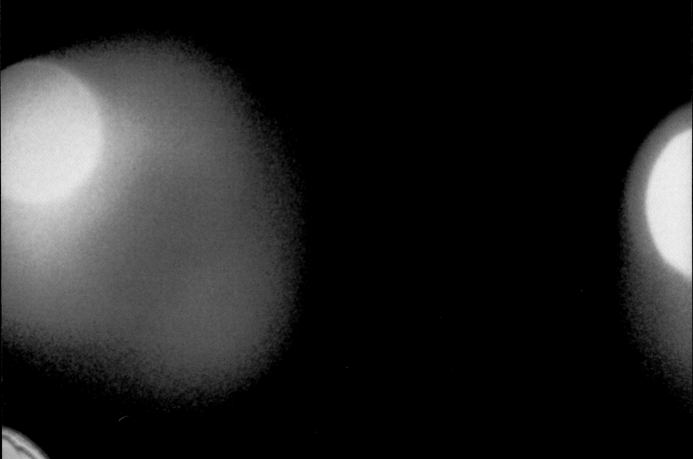

"There's no question I would not have been allowed to work along the lines I've gone if I'd stayed in the band. On the other hand, without me they've all come out of themselves a bit more."

– Peter Gabriel

And then there was one. I remember the chill after first hearing Peter Gabriel's solo material. It was just at the beginning of his work he was calling "music for the '80s." But this was more about future *shock* than it was about the future.

In one piece he was the urban guerrilla planning an assassination. His voice was a dry rasp as he hoped "they" wouldn't see him or his gun. In another, he was the terrorist-intruder, snipping telephone wires. The games he describes are war games. For him, "a normal life" is found in sanitoriums.

Back then he was conjuring up an image of "police room 619," in which South African anti-apartheid leader, Steven Biko, was killed. Yet as the song chants on he then sings about how one man may be stopped but not a movement.

When Gabriel left Genesis in the mid-1970s, many critics assumed the band would suffer, but not him. Wasn't he, after all, not just the voice of the band but its very symbol as well?

During his retreat to the country this early critical reaction reversed itself — not entirely something new for early critical reaction. The better the band did, and the longer he was away, the more it was assumed that it was his career that had reached a dead end. But he began touring in earnest and by the early 1980s he began to reach the critics again.

A critic for *Sounds Magazine* called one of those early performances "one of the best half-dozen rock concerts I've ever seen"; another, from the *New Musical Express*, went on to explain why: "Peter Gabriel is an authority. He knows it and he's using his position, with immense intelligence."

So who was this capital-A authority with the mind of one of Robert Ludlum's spy heroes for intercontinental intrigues?

Like his old mates he grew up warm and comfortably and yet somehow unsettled. He was born, like Tony and Mike, in 1950; the Beatles and the early 1960s became his training ground as much as the field around Cable House, the private prep school he went to, or Charterhouse.

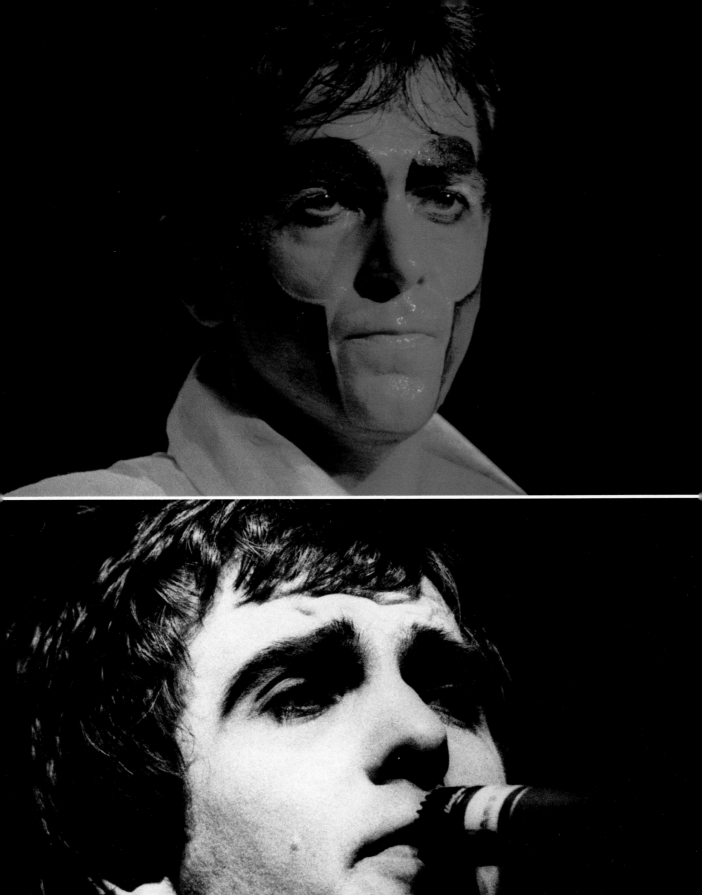

Friends from back then can still remember the beauty of his choirboy's voice. No one expected this young man, who quit one of England's most successful progressive bands, to become the ghostly figure who appeared on rock stages in the 1980s after having worked his way down *through* the crowd with a hand-held light.

Ironically, the singer who wanted to become tougher and who conceived the character, Rael, for *The Lamb Lies Down on Broadway* — the quintessential tough city kid — finally found the toughness he was after — in his ideas.

"There might be political pieces on an album or on the tour," I remember him telling me over the phone from his home in England just prior to his 1980 tour, "but that should not indicate that I am particularly political.

"I'm a communicator. I feel compelled as a communicator to project ideas and images. I'm a good friend of Tom Robinson [the British rocker who, among other things, has performed for homosexual rights organizations and a variety of causes on the left] and I saw how his career went — how he became so readily identified with certain causes that he was exploited by them."

And he was not about to be exploited — even if it cost him. He felt then that everyone involved with Genesis had benefited from the break-up: "There's no question I would not have been allowed to work along the lines I've gone if I'd stayed in the band. On the other hand, without me they've all come out of themselves a bit more, with each one of them, particularly Phil Collins, contributing more on his own."

During the following years his own performing style was honed down to an eerie simplicity. But this, with his schoolboy short hair and the neutral, one-piece uniform he often wears — and sweatsuit, maybe — became as much of a mask as any of the elaborate stagings he'd used in the past with Genesis.

This hard simplicity is a style — like his new music — that comes from rock's progressive edge, not from its mainstream. And as a result he always has to sell it one way or another. One solo album was turned down initially for distribution in North America and was only picked up again after it started to sell well in Europe.

To complicate matters — at least in terms of commercial success — are his associations. He's recorded such progressive musicians as Robert Fripp, Paul Weller, XTC's Dave Gregory, as well as singer Kate Bush, Phil Collins and synthesizer player Larry Fast, who's been included in most of his tour bands. He's also recorded with Laurie Anderson. As impressive as all of these connections might be musically, it doesn't add up to instant huge sales for the record business.

But then again, it's people such as these and Gabriel who are at the heart of the new rock. "I was able to use their talent for certain special reasons," Gabriel added. "For my third album, for instance, I decided that I should re-think the entire song writing process.

"Usually I approached the music from the aspect of melodies and harmonies and filled out the rest later. But Larry Fast suggested I work from a particular rhythm, that it was the backbone of the music which could be fleshed out later.

"So for one song — *Lead a Normal Life*, for instance — the initial rhythmic idea came from a Bo Diddley rhythm and I added to it. I found I could experiment on top of that basic idea, and I could ask the musicians with me to experiment too. I asked the drummers not to use cymbals, for instance. Now, if I were in a band, I could never ask the drummer to do that. But I wanted a certain primitive feel to the music and it was necessary to have that sound.

"I feel I come from the fringe of rock and this allows for a certain change in attitude. I think the same thing happens with every generation of musicians. They come in full of energy and then, later on, want to experiment more. John Lydon is a perfect example of this, as he's now trying some very progressive music. For me, the new attitude and the need to experiment have made me more concerned with the world out there.

"That's why there are the songs about politics, and about everything else. It's just about what's happening."

With him, rock takes a huge leap somewhere else. No one — and certainly not Gabriel himself — knows where exactly. One thing's sure: it's away from whichever comfortable groove or rut he may have found in it.

But let's understand the nature of his experiment. It's not a safe or easy experiment, but it is well within the mainstream. The instruments he uses are both ancient and completely modern: Ghanaian drums and Polymoog synthesizers; marimbas and *musique concrete*. He talks about portable technologies and unheard-of sound syntheses. Yet he knows that what all of this is about is frustration. It comes from his need to expand his own idea of what rock music can be.

He left Genesis because he felt his music was constricted — "my life, too," he said shortly after the split-up — and he began to work with Toronto producer, Bob Ezrin, on what he hoped was a new kind of music.

It was. But it wasn't until the release of his fourth album that a broader public seemed to understand what he's been up to.

And that proved to be quite simple, really; an attempt to give western pop music a new basis.

"You see, the Chinese have a word for danger which is the same as the word for opportunity. I think that when I've actually gone into the things that I've most wanted to avoid, I've got the most out of them."

— *Peter Gabriel*

Ironically, Gabriel, with all his experiments, and Genesis, with all its mainstream success, have more musically in common than they did years ago. After all these years apart Genesis and Gabriel are coming closer and closer together in the mid-'80s.

Genesis' new rhythmic thrust is being matched by

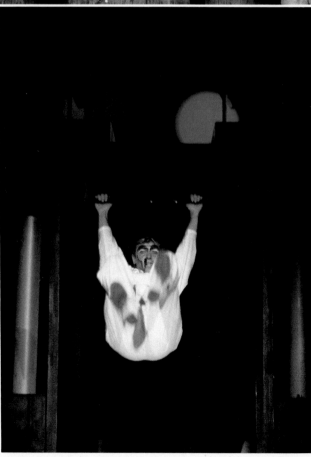

Gabriel's use of various African rhythms and synthesized rhythms. Where the two approaches converge, he insists, is in the source — all these rhythms met in America.

"A lot of rock stuff originated in Africa, like the Bo Diddely rhythm," he was telling me several years and tours after those early "music of the '80s" days. "Most R & B bands didn't realize this rhythm was a straight lift from an African rhythm. I think there's lots of stuff for rock people to feed off — even though they're doing so at a superficial level or on a naive level. That doesn't really matter. What does matter is that there's a lot of stuff that can challenge the way we do things."

A key instrument in facilitating these challenges is the Fairlight computerized synthesizer. With this he is able to reproduce natural sound electronically. He took the Fairlight into scrapheaps and factories, recording anything and everything that moved and made a noise doing it. And he blended this electronic mélange in with the sounds of real instruments.

"I've started using, for instance, a big Brazilian bass drum, which actually belongs to Phil," he says. "The way we were using it was the way we'd use a rock bass drum. It was placed where a rock bass drum would be placed. But it sounds very different. It's a big, full, fat sound, like a military bass drum..."

....*Thunk, thunk!*, he goes with his hands....

He's passing through Toronto only hours before he has to catch an airplane to England. But time stands still the more we talk about rhythm.

"Yeah that's how it goes, the way it was used in *Biko,*" he says. "And there are many more ways to build up exciting rhythms. There is in a lot of ethnic music these tremendously complex patterns. In a sense, they're often fairly simple units but there's a lot of interaction between them. And you can get a tension from that."

This is a look into the unknown, I tell him. North Americans or Europeans are not used to thinking of music, or its rhythms, the way he's trying to see them. We tend to use rhythm as part of a system; it's background for something else, or a part of something else and its overall effect is pleasure whereas the organization of African rhythm is often for informational purposes. It isn't meant to be a beat. It's meant to bring the news.

"Yeah," he says, "and often drums are used for melody. They become the melody. But the way that I like to use it is just to trigger ideas and alternatives and challenges in my music. I don't think that, without ten or fifteen years of involvement, you can actively engross yourself in another culture's music or another person's conscience. What you can do is take little things from this music to work with. That's what I'm doing.

"I have a track on an album [a piece called *Rhythm of the Heat*] which came out of a conversation I was having with a friend. We were talking about white people reacting to black music and vice versa. And he mentioned the story of Carl Jung in Africa — about Jung's reaction to Africa.

"I tried to deal with that in one lyric. The lyric is about memories, dreams, reflections. In his book,

there's a description of his visit to the Sudan where he came across a particular tribe. They started lighting a fire and drumming and dancing, and he self-consciously joined in. They were waving spears. And he went into the middle of it and gradually became totally engrossed and possessed by this thing.

"And he really frightened himself; so much so, in fact, that he went round to all the drummers trying to persuade them to stop. He was shouting at them. Jung himself was shouting at all the drummers. And started offering them money and pins and thimbles and anything that he had to try and get them to stop.

"What a strong image this is. There was this great Western thinker actually going out there and having something — the shadow — take control."

There's danger here, a kind of intellectual risk-taking that he seems to know can take him out of his depth. For all his gentleness, the images he himself creates, both in his lyrics or for the screen, are horrific.

The scare is built right into the nature of his music. The video for *Shock the Monkey* has a kind of grotesque, pallid, futuristic look to it. Oh, he has a very rational explanation too for it all. He has a very rational explanation for everything. But that doesn't take away the shock.

"Hmmm," says Gabriel. "You see, the Chinese have a word for danger which is the same as the word for opportunity. I think that when I've actually gone into the things that I've most wanted to avoid, I've got the most out of them.

"There's obviously a certain amount of fashion in this current interest in African music right now. There are lots of people doing it. But this is not new. There's this long tradition in rock, and particularly jazz, to look to other cultures, especially African. And I think that even when the fashion is gone and interest has gone elsewhere, a lot of Third World influence is going to grow in Western society anyway.

"I think the more interaction there is the better everything will be. And as long as we can bring different kinds of music to the festivals and things like that, we can encourage more interaction. I don't mean interaction in a loose jamming sense, but in somewhat controlled situations in order that they will stand up to repeated listening.

"I really think that we can develop a sort of a merger between these outside influences and high-tech. When it comes to finding new directions, high-tech has been it so far. But it's got this cold, dehumanizing image and I think that the second generation of technology is now coming through which is much more flexible, much more passive and, yes, usable. It'll be much more user responsive.

"You'll be able to use this new kind of technology as a much more sensitive and emotive coloring device than you had been able to previously. You won't have to record all sorts of musical instruments and go into scrapyards and sort through paving stones and exhaust pipes, and make tunnel noises to get the sounds you want.

"You'll get a big library of sound. It'll be like a play-land that you can go into. You'll be able to just treat things as sounds. You'll be able to forget about where they came from and how you got them.

"This stuff is absurdly expensive right now, but I'm sure — and I know the people who make these things as well as some of the other things — these types of options will be available. I am convinced that in a few years virtually every home will have its home computer, and the kind of music-making thing I'm talking about will be an attachment that will also be as common in every home as a piano.

"And in the same way recording will be evolution-ized. Five or ten years ago you had to go to a physically controlled studio and work with a professional engineer. That was the only way to make a record.

"But that's going to be changed too. So you'll bring a studio into your bedroom and you'll get your tape released on vinyl — or in England you'll get it played on radio the week after you've finished with it.

"That process will be demystifying. To actually be able to make records with lots of rich and interesting sounds that process will soon be available to everyone. It may take five years to happen. But I think it's very exciting to think about because when it does happen it will change the idea of who a musician is.

"As of now we categorize musicians and non-musi-cians as those who can play and those who can't play. In the future it'll be those who want to play and those who don't want to play.

"I don't think you'll ever replace the craftsmanship that a good musician has — or the relationship that one person has with his instrument over many years. But what will happen is that other people — anyone — will have access to all the sounds anyone would want."

If this playpen of sound were available to everyone what we might end up with is not music per se, at least not music as we think of it now, but an entirely new kind of art based on sound. Maybe poets will stage a comeback?

"Okay, let's call it sound rather than music," he goes on. "I think that there's a lot that people could do with all this sound: they could refresh themselves in sound.

"I do that now. If I feel really miserable I can go and sit down at the piano and come away half an hour later feeling a lot better. So if all the musical possibilities were increased that aspect of the thing would be great.

"In general, I think that people should grab the technology and make sure it works for them — to enable them to fulfil more things within them. That way the technology won't be used against them.

"I think there's a radical change in our world: a change which will affect theories, Marxist theories or whatever, which are based on exploitation of labor and physical work. When machines can do physical work better and cheaper than people, then that particular type of exploitation — the exploitation of labor — will cease because it's economically stupid.

"Maybe the shift is away from money to information. What's dividing the rich and the poor is no longer just money — they're information divided."

PART FIVE
GENESIS ON GENESIS

"There's a special feel to their music."

– *Chester Thompson*

There are those people who think of Genesis as being somehow still involved with Steve Hackett. Peter's leaving was so well publicized, the break has always seemed more absolute than it was. By contrast, Steve just drifted away, it seemed.

Did his recording a solo album, *Voyage of the Acolyte*, early on underline the split? Wasn't there a lot of talk about the others doing solo albums around the same time?

Things had been blurred. So much was happening. Critics and fans were worried whether the band could survive without Gabriel when in truth it was having also to learn how to survive without this sensitive guitarist who'd been with the band through the formative early albums, joining the band in 1970 and staying with it for almost seven years.

Hackett left, he said, because he felt his music was being overlooked by the band. He wanted to record o‍ his own. His second album, *Please Don't Touch*, arrive‍ in April, 1978 — two months before Peter Gabriel‍ second album, *Peter Gabriel*, was released.

One afternoon, after having talked with Tony, Mik‍ and Phil, I found myself with Chester Thompson. Th‍ drummer had come to the band late in 1976, not lon‍ before Hackett was to leave. (Bill Bruford had been ‍ temporary drummer after Collins was pressed int‍ action as the singer and front man). Thompson was a‍ alumnus of Weather Report and Frank Zappa. He wa‍ soon joined by Daryl Stuermer, the guitarist fro‍ Milwaukee who'd been with George Duke and Jean‍ Luc Ponty.

Daryl and I spoke recently, too, about how he cam‍ to join Genesis.

"Why did I take the gig? I think the reason I took it ‍ after hearing a Genesis album called *A Trick of the Ta*‍ Jean-Luc Ponty had played. In fact, he pinpointed ‍ certain song that he liked called *Squonks*, and what h‍ liked about that one was the feel — which was obviousl‍ Phil's drum beat — and basically the composition of th‍ songs.

"I had met Chester Thompson at O'Hara Airport i‍ Chicago. I had known Chester before, but he was o‍ tour at this time with *The Wiz* and I was with Jean-Lu‍ Ponty, and he said that he was going to be joining th‍

group Genesis. My impression of Genesis at that time was something that I'd seen on a television show maybe five years previous which was Peter Gabriel and Mike Love from the Beach Boys and John McLaughlin and Charles Lloyd and there was an interview show by a guy named Chip Munk.

"So those four musicians were on and I was mainly watching the show to see Charles Lloyd and John McLaughlin — I didn't know anything about Peter Gabriel. At the time I thought the group Genesis was a group maybe like Rush, or something like that, which wasn't really the kind of music that I listen to. They showed a part from a film clip or video of Genesis, live with Peter Gabriel from *Supper's Ready*. It was the point where Peter was wearing the outfits and the flower. I think they were doing a part from *Willow Farm*.

"So my first impression of Genesis was that they were more of a theatrical group, and I was into more of the fusion side of jazz-rock at the time, playing with Jean-Luc Ponty. So that's what I thought Genesis was all about. And it was only a short segment that I saw.

"And then, when I met Chester at the airport in Chicago and he said he was going to join the band, I thought, that's strange, I can't picture him in that group. Chester had played with Weather Report and Frank Zappa and I thought, well, maybe at least Zappa was a little bit closer to that kind of music, but not even that close.

"Jean-Luc Ponty just so happened to, on that tour, play me that song, *Squonks*, so that gave me a better impression of what Genesis was all about. I thought I would listen to the whole tape so I asked Jean-Luc if I could borrow it. On that tour I listened to them. It brought back memories of when I was younger — when I was listening to groups like King Crimson and Procul Harum and even the Moody Blues at that time. But they were like a modern-day King Crimson, Moody Blues, Procul Harum. They gave me some of that same feeling. And I really like those kind of groups. They were almost, in a sense, a rock band but they were more poetic and sophisticated. So I had quite a good impression after I listened to *A Trick of the Tail*.

"Then about a year later after Chester had joined the group — I hadn't seen the group yet — I got a call. They were looking for a guitar player and at that time I had been playing with Jean-Luc Ponty for about three years and I was about ready for a change. So I thought I'd give that a try because I was recommended to the group. I went to New York and met Mike Rutherford, and in fact, a little bit before that, they had sent me a tape to listen to — *Squonks* and a song called *Down and Out* — and two other songs which I can't remember right now. I liked the songs very much. So I learned the songs and I went for the audition. Basically Mike said, 'I think this will work out,' and he said 'I'll have to call you at six o'clock at your hotel because I have to audition four other guitar players' even though he thought it would work out with me.

"Then I called my wife on the phone and I told her, 'I think I have a gig.' And I wasn't sure that I wanted it. I didn't know if I wanted the gig because I didn't think I would have enough to do as a guitar player. The songs that they gave me to listen to and the songs I heard on record — a lot of times you couldn't even tell what the guitar was playing. A lot of times it sounded more like a synthesizer and, in fact, Steve Hackett actually played quite like a synthesizer player sometimes. I mean, his sounds were very unusual. I should actually say they were more unusual than a synthesizer. And you couldn't tell if it was really guitar playing — you didn't hear the typical guitar sounds so you didn't know if the guitar was really doing that much. At the same time I came from a background of playing more guitar solos — in Jean-Luc Ponty's band and also in the band that I was in before that. So I didn't know if I was going to have enough to do.

"But then I decided that I would give this a shot because it was something different for me and I could probably learn something. So I did do it. It was also paying a lot more than the group that I had played with before and also I thought it would give me more exposure as a guitar player.

"So all those were good reasons to do it. So I did it and found out that I had a lot more to do than I thought — playing bass pedals and I learned more about sounds than I would have if I had've stayed in the jazz fusion vein."

Did he think that his arrival and Chester's arrival to the band changed things?

"I think sometimes we don't realize what influence we have over each other in many ways. That's why it's hard to say whether it was because we joined the band that they felt something else from the music — or felt the way we played the music was somehow different. Or perhaps they were just going to go in that direction anyway. We don't really know. They could open their minds to maybe even listen to some other things. I don't know.

"I think it was gradual. I don't think they changed immediately. You can see the progression into the more contemporary music. I think when they did *And Then There Were Three*, that was kind of a change right there obviously just because there were only three of them. But I thought the next record, *Duke*, to me, said that they were going to get into this more contemporary sound, or be more American-sounding than they were before. And I think that had a lot to do with Phil's influence, I don't know why. It's always hard for us to figure out why this has all happened. But actually I like the change because maybe that's more my background.

"It seems to me that they're going to be changing all the time. I don't know what the next step is going to be. My favorite album is *Abacab*. I think that really shows how diverse they are."

The point is this: Thompson and Stuermer have been with Genesis as long as Hackett had been. Yet the drummer, at least, still finds himself able to be something of the outsider looking at the three originals.

"There's a special feel to their music," Chester Thompson was telling me. "It's something I had to find out playing with them — and by getting to know them.

"They've covered an awful lot of territory since I'v

been in the band. Since '77, it's been. They have a real instinctive feel. The best thing I think they've got going for them is that they're relatively uneducated musically — you know, as far as the formal training point of view. And with that comes a bit more freedom. I think they're more free to express ideas than others might be. In other words, they don't know the rules which say you shouldn't do this and you shouldn't do that.

"Some of their earlier stuff probably did seem a bit classically oriented which was sort of the trademark of the whole progressive thing in those days anyway. That's changed, of course. But there are some things which haven't. I've been here long enough now that, even in the new music, I can always hear where they're coming from.

"It's their way of doing things. If you divide a song into sections — like *Abacab*, which has the structure A-B-A-C — you are working with the parts of a song and how they're put together. Well, they've got certain ways of doing it. There's a certain thing about the way they put songs together and that hasn't changed very much at all.

"Whatever the components of the song are, half of the battle is knowing in what order to put them. There's a talent to being able to hear what complements which, what is a climax, what's an anti-climax. That's a different kind of gift and they have it.

"When I first joined the band, Tony and Mike didn't take themselves all that seriously as players. They said that all those years they'd been more concerned with just being writers and being able to play what they had written rather than trying to be hotshot players. But lately, it seems that they have taken their playing quite a bit more seriously."

But is it their individually arrived-at styles that give the band its signature? Chester thinks he could distinguish Genesis from other bands just "by the kind of chords Tony plays."

"I don't know what to call these chords. They're pretty simple actually. He's got a lovely way of spreading them out so that things tend to sound bigger than they really are. To sit along and try and play along with the songs is a lot simpler than I would have ever dreamed, actually. I mean, at the keyboard. I can play the basic chords and all that. But the way he voices the chords is completely his own thing.

"There's a certain feel that Mike has when he's playing guitar or bass but especially when he's playing the bass. He's got a real unique feel so the minute you hear it you know it's him.

"Phil's sound is in his feel as well but he's probably most recognized for his sound more than anything these days.

"As for me, I'm into variety. I'm not a jazz drummer or a rock drummer. I mean, I can do all of that but don't identify myself with any one particular style.

"But in the last few years since I've been with Genesis the most consistent comment I've heard is that it's actually become more percussion-heavy than guitar-heavy and that certainly makes it different from most rock bands."

Here too, I point out, is another reason why the new

Genesis is a far more rhythmic band. With Chester and Daryl, two Americans grounded in jazz, the rhythmic input increased dramatically. Now there's a band with a drummer up front and at back.

"When I first joined I was there basically to do onstage what Phil did on the records — you know, to play his parts when he was up front singing. The records sell because the kids have come to expect some sort of consistency between what they hear on them and how things are done onstage. So that's what the band tries to do. They try to keep the stage sound pretty consistent with what's on record. What changes are made or happen between the two are natural changes. There's never been a conscious attempt to do something onstage differently than what is on record.

"The music seems to be naturally moving in this new direction, though. I think as you become more mature, musically you become more economical in your playing. You find you can accomplish a lot more with a lot fewer notes. You find a piece doesn't have to be fifteen minutes long — that you can say what you want to say in four or five minutes.

"That was the difference for me between playing with Zappa and with Weather Report. With Zappa, I

learned how to play every sort of complicated music. With Weather Report I learned when to leave stuff out — when not to play.

"With Genesis, I'm learning something about writing. That's one thing I'm particularly interested in — writing. I've learned an awful lot from them about writing because that's one of their strong points."

A small, portable computer, all buttons and slides and compact technology, sits in one corner. It goes out on tours with him. He explains how he's programming some of his songs into it right now. He's thinking about recording his own album.

We talk about drummers. And I tell him that I think Phil has never been as well recognized as he should be as a drummer. Maybe it's because he's such an economical player, that he's not flashy.

"He's real musical," says Chester. "He's one of the most musical drummers around. He's more interested in complementing the music around him than doing something that's real flash.

"As for what I'm doing for my own music, well, I don't do Genesis at all in what I do. The only similarity between what I might write and what Genesis does comes from the fact that I like the idea of things that change in the middle — where there's a sudden change in the music. That's the way some of their stuff goes.

"When I write, I like to totally go off the beaten path for a bit. But that's an *approach* to writing. The musical elements I choose to use are things that are natural to me. They are far removed from what Genesis might use. There might be a similarity in structure, perhaps.

"I think this change of pattern has almost become their musical signature. You can hear it even in their new stuff. Even though it's a lot more straight ahead than it used to be, there is still going to be some sort of deviation where the music's going to change and go in a slightly different direction for a while.

"It doesn't happen all the time. But in most cases, especially wherever it's needed, there is always that little deviation, that change of direction."

"I get the impression," I tell him, "that they are very straight ahead, small-C conservative people."

"Yeah," he says, "they're pretty straight. Working with them has always been a real pleasant situation to be in. Everybody's pretty straight ahead. And that's a good thing, I think. I feel for those who try to live the rock'n'roll image. I'm sure we're all a bit looser on the road than we are at home. But you just can't live like that all the time.

"Some do, I know. And sure, on the road there are later nights and maybe a drink or two more than you would have had at home. But here everybody's got families. Everybody's into their families.

"Phil is, as you probably know, the workaholic in the band. But even as a workaholic, he's not a maniac. It's just that that happens to be his pace — his natural pace. Actually, I don't see him as any sort of extremist at all. Workaholics tend to be a bit extreme. With him it's pretty balanced.

"But that's the way it is with everybody here. Everybody's a good person. Everybody's image is not wrapped up in some sort of rock'n'roll style."

Understanding Genesis may have been difficult over the years: what did all those early songs mean? Why were people quitting? Why did they go on? Why the change to what they're doing now?

What hasn't been difficult is getting a feel for the band itself; for those in it, and for what they felt.

The more Chester talked about Genesis, the easier it was for me to see that he had an attachment to these people and that, as cautious as he might be in talking about it with an outsider, it is very much for real.

"I learned a long time ago when I was working with Zappa," he goes on, "that if I'm going to be playing other people's music — and I want to continue doing that because I like the variety — it's best that I have outlets of my own. If I have my own projects it makes me much more effective to do the work for other people. Otherwise it would become really frustrating for me. Something would blow up inside me. This, working with Genesis, leaves me plenty of time to pursue my own efforts and gives me plenty of family time.

"It's not that I'm part of the band. Definitely not. When we're on tour...well, *then* you're part of the band. Then there's that sense that you know you've got a job to do and that everybody's got to hold up their end as well. Everybody has to be sensitive to what everybody else is doing. So in that sense, it's a band. In rehearsal there's always that transition when one day it starts sounding like a band again.

"But I do realize that part of my value to them is that it doesn't bother me not to be in the band. Like there was the time when Phil was in Brand X. One of the reasons he stopped doing things with Brand X was because no drummers were willing to take the gig unless they were going to do the records. Nobody was willing to come in and fill in on a job where there wasn't that much glory. And there certainly wasn't a lot of money involved. Just to come in to fill someone else's shoes — well, no one wanted that.

"A lot of guys are really career-oriented these days and they're just not going to go along with this kind of thing. A lot of guys are going to say, 'Hell, if I'm doing the records I want to do the tour.'

"I guess you could say this is a stepping stone to something else for me. But I don't know. I've been here for almost seven years. It's an awfully wide stepping stone.

"But that brings up the business about career again. Everybody is so career-oriented it's ridiculous, especially around Los Angeles. There are times you think they're almost forgetting about the music itself. But I have to watch that as well. Sometimes you can get so caught up in your career that you forget what a joy it is to play music. I think that feeling needs to be first in your mind.

"Obviously, you've got to do it for a living. It's what you choose to do. You're not going to spend twenty-two years in music and then try to go out and get an accounting job. There are standards. I do have to maintain a sort of professional posture about it all.

"But at the same time I won't do a gig I don't like. And if I don't like the music or I feel I really can't be around the people — and I have yet to find a situation where I couldn't be around the people — I won't do it. I couldn't do any gig just for the money.

"Probably, except the executive positions, this is one of the higher paying professions around, I would imagine. Well, you've got sports but that's a pretty short-lived career.

"But I've been doing what I do for...let's see, I got my first steady gig, a real working-steady, every-weekend situation in 1962. I was thirteen. Okay, so I've got over twenty-one working years at this now. I think that anyone with over twenty-one years' experience at anything should be getting paid. You've achieved something that's become something of worth in your profession. Besides, there weren't that many shortcuts in getting to what you're worth.

"You can get situations where a band, a young band where everyone is a teenager, can end up with a record deal. They get a hit and everything happens pretty fast for them. But I think they'll find they are probably in for some pretty stormy roads ahead of them.

"But then there's Genesis, fifteen albums later and doing better than ever."

We talk some more then say goodbye, and I head

down the street, listening through my earphones to the tape of the three insiders talking among themselves — about themselves.

We'd been chatting in the backstage dressing room. The tape had been left on. It was Genesis on Genesis.

And as they talked, for the time I was forgotten.

"You can make a record on your own and you can choose to do other things. It's a question of choices. We all choose to be in a group."

– Phil Collins

And still there are three.

"We could have become tired, worn out," says Mike. "I think playing in a group, especially live, with all the sound checks and all the rest, does teach you to be able to handle on-the-spot type situations and stay calm. We don't tend to fly off the handle any more. You know, I used to."

"We're here to play," says Phil. "That's it, basically..."

"It's been a very gradual thing for us and I think we've had to adjust from year to year to each new situation," Tony continues, straightening up on the equipment box he's sitting on. "We'll always feel, in terms of our careers, that we're still pressing. We still feel we're pressing with our music, too. But that's another story. From a career point of view we still have a long way to go."

Mike looks at him: "For quite a while, for each new album we did, there was someone leaving or someone who was going through a big change. Suddenly, for one new album no one was leaving. And that worked because we thrive on our talents. The next time around there was the challenge of producing ourselves and using our own studio which we had built."

Tony: "I do think it's a matter of time. Over a period of time your tastes change and things you want to do change as well. There's a lot of areas of music we've never covered which we would enjoy doing."

Mike: "It's quite possible we might not be here today had the others not left. You never know where we would have gone."

Tony: "I never felt the course of the band changed all that much. It depended on how strong the influence of the person leaving had been on a particular album. But as great an influence as anyone was up to the point they left the band, I don't think their going changed us all that much."

Mike: "There's never ever been one big single, one

big hit that suddenly changed our status or popularity in the country. There have been surges of popularity over the years, but there's never ever been the great roaring up-from-nowhere thing."

"The same thing when we first started," says Phil looking at the other two. "It was gradual at first, from clubs to colleges to universities, from supporting two or three bands in a concert tour to our *own* tour to the big gigs. It was the same thing in America; unless you've got the groundwork there, you won't get the kind of fans you need. You know, one minute they'll like your album and they'll like the band but the next week they'll like somebody else. We've had such a lot of groundwork done in America since 1972."

Tony: "I think a lot of it depends on the live thing. We've always seemed to have done better live than our record sales would suggest. And this has been true at every point in our career. In England particularly, it was our reputation from the live shows more than the records themselves which helped us. We never got played on the radio in England at all really up until 1978. And yet our records have been selling really well in England for about four or five years previous."

Did they ever think about this longevity — that they were growing old? I asked.

There's some shuffling and a bit of a pause, then Tony: "Yeah, well, I think we have a lot of young people in the audiences these days. I think that's the only way to remain a fresh group. Rock music, when it first appeared, was very much for young people. I don't think it has to remain like that. I think anyone can like it. And more and more I feel that a whole range of ages is liking it."

Phil: "That's good for us, I think. We're not writing for people of just our own age. We're writing music that we like to write. And it is also obviously palatable to the thireen-, fourteen-, and fifteen-year-old kids who buy records."

Mike: "We do think about where we're going all the time. Every year. Each year we think about the chance of going on forever and ever. I think that every time you make an album you make a commitment — if the album works and the writing works, then you get excited about still working together. Mentally you commit yourself with each new album you're doing and with whatever goes with it, the touring or promoting and the making it happen. And the next time around you sort of just wait and see what'll happen *then....*"

Phil: "There are so many different aspects to it all. But I like to think of it as just three people getting together to write some music. That can continue until we don't enjoy it. But there's no point in having any kind of deadline where the band has to stop. I hope to be carrying on as long as we actually want to, really."

Mike: "For the last couple of albums we've gotten back much more to writing group material. We'd lost that bit for a while. We were doing many more individual songs. When we write together it's like improvisation. Some songs have only a little bit to start with — maybe just a couple of chords. And then something just happens. You're playing together, you're jamming to-

gether, and something happens. It's a sort of spark. And then there's the next chord and then there's the rhythm. And without saying anything we can all feel that there's something there. Then we take that and it often becomes a bit of a song. But you can't put your finger on exactly how it happens.''

''And that,'' adds Phil quickly, ''is what is so nice about being in a group.''

Tony: ''That's the advantage. That's why we're trying to get back to writing all our stuff as a group. Because that's the most exciting thing about rhythm — when you're in rehearsal and something starts to evolve.''

Phil: ''And you can't do it on your own. It's one thing you can't do. It's great when you realize that things are running well. We want to keep doing songs that you feel very close to. There is nothing like...well, throwing something up in the air, some musical idea, something maybe you tried to finish but weren't able to, and have someone else take it and say 'oh, yeah, yeah,' and make you see it in a different light....''

''...Yeah, and it's great,'' Mike adds in quickly, ''when you've got a certain bit or riff going and someone does something to it, plays along with it in such a different way that you think, 'What are they doing?' But then suddenly it all sort of jells...''

''That's why people leave groups,'' says Phil firmly. ''They don't want to be part of that process any more.''

Tony: ''Also, we're trying to get into a situation where we can carry through our own ideas outside the group as well, so that you can be in charge of the whole situation if you like, and so that you can follow through with an idea in the way you actually saw it. Obviously there comes the time when another guy will do your bit of music in a different way than you'd expected. And maybe it's great, maybe it's not. But there's no telling how good it might be unless you yourself had actually followed it through in the way you'd originally seen it. You get a chance to do that as an individual.''

Phil: ''I think we all find out about these differences in our ideas when we do interviews together. Otherwise we don't talk about it much. Like these solo careers — I don't think of them as 'solo careers' because solo generally means that you are not with the group as opposed to just making a record that you happen to make. You can make a record on your own and you can choose to do other things. It's a question of choices. We all choose to be in a group. We needn't be in a group but we choose to be in a group. We do these different projects. We do film soundtracks. We produce other people. I see the individual thing developing alongside the group thing. Then there's no conflict of interest.''

Mike: ''I seriously think that if we hadn't started working outside of the group, we might not be here. I think we've needed that. Some people do it because they're not happy with what they're doing in the group. And they go off on their own and that makes them happy. Whereas with us, it's just that we all write quite a lot and we need other outlets. One album a year in the group isn't enough. With all the solo stuff, you don't arrive with a suitcase full of songs for that one group outlet each year — you've probably done something on your own. And you're looking forward to

working with other people and bouncing ideas around.''

Phil: "A lot of groups are dictatorships. Most groups have a leader or a single writer and that is why other people tend to do solo albums. And as soon as they get a glimmer of success on their own, it's 'Right, I'm off on my own.' But we work very differently than that.''

"This year's album is 'us' this year. And if next year the chemistry among the three of us is good and it takes us somewhere else, we'll go there."

– Mike Rutherford

It's pointed out that Tony Smith, their manager, has suggested that boarding school, no matter how traumatic or wonderful the experience, created a special bond.

Tony: "Mike and I weren't friends at school. We hardly knew each other really..."

"...Isn't that the original reason why groups get together?" says Phil. "Because you're mates? And you do it because you like listening to records together?"

Mike: "It holds together basically because of the musical enjoyment, the musical respect and the sort of chemistry that works. That's what holds it together."

Tony: "But it's all down to luck, really — the whole thing. Phil wasn't one of the original 'friends' if you like. We got him as a professional. It was all sorts of chance happenings over the years that made the thing what it is. There's so much luck involved in it all — as well as a lot of hard work."

Phil: "You come to appreciate that one person covers an area that you don't. And that's why you respect him. It's not as if we can all do everything about the same. There are certain things you have to trust each other to do."

Mike: "We work very well because there's no sort of taboo areas any more. That wasn't the way it was going back a few years. It used to be, well, the drums are his and the keyboards are his and I was on the bass. It was all very territorial. Whereas now, especially because we're producing our material, there are no little corners where no one can come in and offer suggestions. If somebody really feels strongly about an idea or a part they've got then he'll hang onto it and follow it through. That's why I think it works with us producing ourselves. It wouldn't have worked a few years ago. But we reached the way of working together."

Tony: "It's impossible to fight when you produce yourselves..." — he stops to think for a second, then goes on — "...it's also helped to have challenges. Peter leaving us was a challenge for us and obviously we found we had the confidence in ourselves so that we

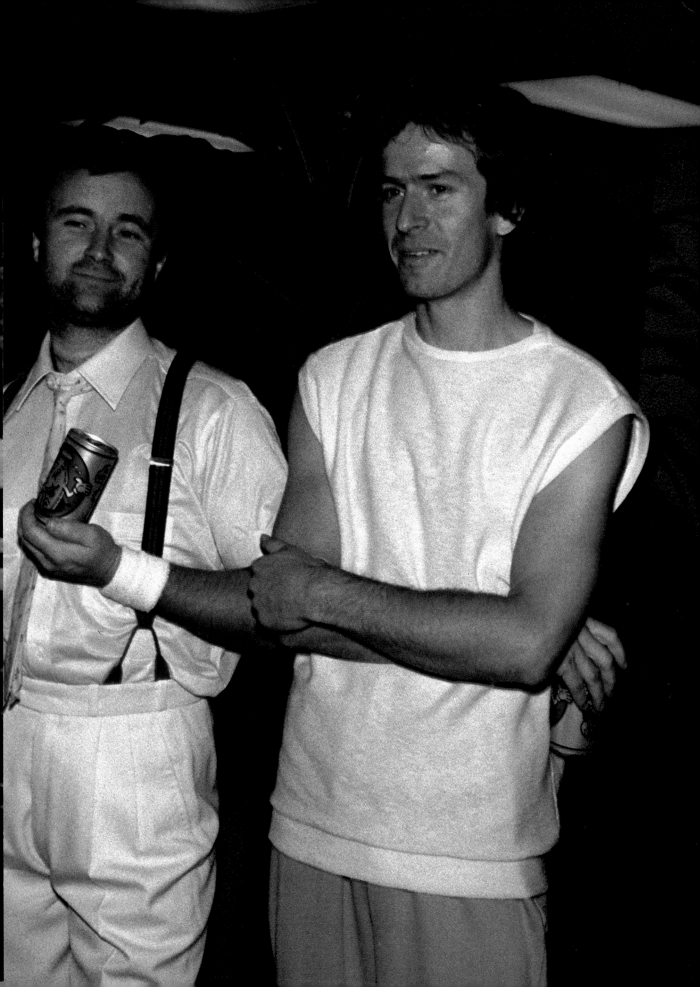

could easily carry on — as long as by losing Peter we weren't losing so much of our image that the audience would leave us as a result. But what we found was that in fact the audience was prepared to give us a big chance. *A Trick of the Tail* was a fortunate album. It was both like the previous Genesis material and yet it also had a slightly more commercial edge to it. The combination was very successful at the time. As I say, luck. We couldn't plan that."

Phil: "The fundamental thing has always been the music. I'm sure there are people out there who would lay down their lives thinking that Peter wrote all the music or that he was the basic core of the whole thing. Like *The Lamb*. I mean, I'm sure that people think that Peter wrote all of *The Lamb* or all of *Supper's Ready*, or all of *Watchers of the Sky* — you know, the classic Genesis-type tune. They would be surprised if they actually knew what went on inside the band. It's because of the group effort that we had so much confidence when he left. And we knew that it was just one out of five who'd left. We knew that there were still four people and that the chemistry was still very much alive."

Tony: "Peter's main contribution was as the stage performer. That was the place where he did more than anyone else. As a writer and as a performer on record it was pretty much an equal thing. And so that was another challenge that came our way: could we present ourselves live?"

Mike: "We have changed. We find that particularly when it comes to rehearsing some of the old songs. Lyrics often date more than the music does. Some music dates. But you play some old songs and musically they come to life again. But with the lyrics you find certain phrases and lines that sound dated. I mean that fashions change and you change, so some of the lyrics sound dated."

Tony: "All we've ever done is written to please ourselves. I no longer get a thrill out of writing Roman mythology-type lyrics. It's just after you've done it a lot of times there comes a point where you can't do it again. You see? All we've ever been trying to do is to write music to please ourselves. If we do this, other people will pick up on it as well. We use ourselves as the critics.

"I think we wrote stories about different things because we found it very difficult to write songs about boy-and-girl relationships. This was my case anyhow. I found it much easier to write a story about a couple of wolves. Our self-consciousness probably made it more difficult to write about obvious things in the earlier days. It was much easier to write in a more abstract kind of way. Or else create a story. The great thing about having a story, particularly if you've got a long song, is that you can work all the moods into it and it gives you a beginning and an end. There's an obvious format to use and you can sort of plan it out beforehand. But if you're writing a song which doesn't have a storyline it's often more difficult."

Mike: "At one time we used to read certain kinds of books — certain amounts of fantasy books. Nowadays, I don't read that sort any more. The big thing is change...."

Phil: "...The costumes, for instance, were developed in those days when PA systems weren't very good. So you had to start acting out the songs. You tried to get the audience to understand what they couldn't hear. That explains the stories in between the tunes which a lot of people thought were part of the act. They were in fact there because people had a lot of tuning up to do for the next song. And so with people sitting there in silence Peter started telling stories. There was an evolution from having an awful silence to having something to say to the audience that would make them laugh. It was a good thing to make them laugh because it took them off the edges of their seats."

But weren't the songs and costumes so bizarre that the band seemed to come from someplace outside of rock? Did they feel themselves a part of rock'n'roll?

Tony: "Definitely. It's contemporary music. That's the idea of the kind of music we write and the kind of music everybody else in this business is doing. It's music for that time. If people still like it in five years, that's great. That's a bonus. But that's not really what we're trying to do. It's contemporary music. And I think it should be thought of as that and judged on that, too."

Mike: "It's always been gut for us."

Phil: "I think it's been a lot gutsier than people have thought. Some of the songs that have come out sounding very limp on the albums have been very gutsy in the rehearsal room. We have always felt that we're more of a gut band than the people who just bought the records and listened to them maybe thought we were."

Tony: "We like contrast too. We like the whole spectrum of music from the very soft stuff to very aggressive stuff. I think this aggressive edge has always been there but maybe the production didn't make it come through. You take a song like *Supper's Ready*. It has some very aggressive moments in it as well as some very sweet moments. And that, to me, is what I like — these sorts of contrasts within the group. This is what keeps it interesting for me. I wouldn't ever like to do just one thing."

Mike: "I'm always amazed by the number of people who come to see our shows in England who have Motorhead jackets on or the Clash or AC/DC. There's a side which we do that is very heavy. We do an awful lot more than some think. If you talk to fans, some people will like Genesis for a certain sort of music. The other stuff they don't particularly like so they'll take it or leave it. And yet other persons will be the total reversal of that, and they'll like the softer side, more melodic. I think we draw from a wide audience. But you know, we have actually avoided any sort of master plan. I think many people like all this musical change. This year's album is 'us' this year. And if next year the chemistry among the three of us is good and it takes us somewhere else, we'll go there."

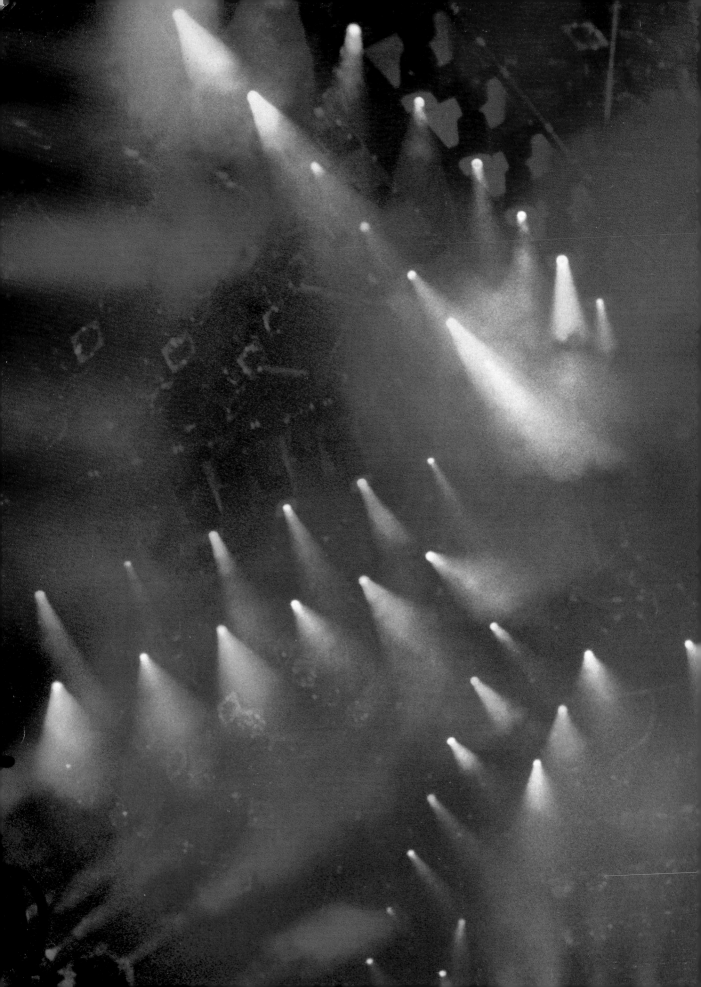

About the Authors

Philip Kamin began photographing rock bands in 1978 when he picked up a camera for the first time and followed Genesis on tour. Since then his photographs have appeared worldwide in magazines, songbooks, programs, publicity campaigns and books, and on album covers and posters. In addition to those groups mentioned in the book list, Philip has also worked with The Cars, The Little River Band, Van Halen, Black Sabbath, Rod Stewart, Teenage Head, Martha And The Muffins, Roxy Music and Ian Dury. A native of Toronto, he makes that city his home.

Philip Kamin uses Canon cameras and equipment exclusively: F1 and A1 bodies with motor drive; lenses: 24mm f/2, 35mm f/2, 50mm f/1.4, 85mm f/1.8, 135mm f/2, 200mm f/2.8, and 300mm f/4 Aspherical, and Canon strobe system.

Peter Goddard is the rock and jazz critic for the *Toronto Star*. He has written for a variety of magazines in Canada, the U.S. and France, and has received a National Newspaper Award for critical writing. Goddard has an M.A. in music and a degree in solo piano performance. He has written several scores for experimental film, including electronic music, and has written and produced for television and radio. Peter, his wife and daughter reside in Toronto, and they spend part of the year on their farm in France. Peter is currently working on a novel, and has been commissioned to write a history of popular music.

Books by Philip Kamin and Peter Goddard

The Rolling Stones Live (In the U.S., *The Rolling Stones: The Last Tour*)
The Who: The Farewell Tour
David Bowie: Out of the Cool
The Police Chronicles
Van Halen

By Philip Kamin and James Karnbach

The Rolling Stones in Europe